CLYMER®

MANUALS

YAMAHA
80-175cc PISTON-PORT • 1968-1976

WHAT'S IN YOUR TOOLBOX?

You Tube™

More information available at Clymer.com
Phone: 805-498-6703

Haynes Publishing Group
Sparkford Nr Yeovil
Somerset BA22 7JJ England

Haynes North America, Inc
859 Lawrence Drive
Newbury Park
California 91320 USA

ISBN-10: 0-89287-235-7
ISBN-13: 978-0-89287-235-0

Chapter One
General Information   1

Chapter Two
Periodic Maintenance   2

Chapter Three
Engine, Transmission and Clutch   3

Chapter Four
Carburetors   4

Chapter Five
Electrical System   5

Chapter Six
Chassis Service   6

Chapter Seven
Troubleshooting   7

Appendix
Specifications   8

Index   9

Wiring Diagrams   10

Common spark plug conditions

NORMAL

Symptoms: Brown to grayish-tan color and slight electrode wear. Correct heat range for engine and operating conditions.
Recommendation: When new spark plugs are installed, replace with plugs of the same heat range.

WORN

Symptoms: Rounded electrodes with a small amount of deposits on the firing end. Normal color. Causes hard starting in damp or cold weather and poor fuel economy.
Recommendation: Plugs have been left in the engine too long. Replace with new plugs of the same heat range. Follow the recommended maintenance schedule.

TOO HOT

Symptoms: Blistered, white insulator, eroded electrode and absence of deposits. Results in shortened plug life.
Recommendation: Check for the correct plug heat range, over-advanced ignition timing, lean fuel mixture, intake manifold vacuum leaks, sticking valves and insufficient engine cooling.

CARBON DEPOSITS

Symptoms: Dry sooty deposits indicate a rich mixture or weak ignition. Causes misfiring, hard starting and hesitation.
Recommendation: Make sure the plug has the correct heat range. Check for a clogged air filter or problem in the fuel system or engine management system. Also check for ignition system problems.

PREIGNITION

Symptoms: Melted electrodes. Insulators are white, but may be dirty due to misfiring or flying debris in the combustion chamber. Can lead to engine damage.
Recommendation: Check for the correct plug heat range, over-advanced ignition timing, lean fuel mixture, insufficient engine cooling and lack of lubrication.

ASH DEPOSITS

Symptoms: Light brown deposits encrusted on the side or center electrodes or both. Derived from oil and/or fuel additives. Excessive amounts may mask the spark, causing misfiring and hesitation during acceleration.
Recommendation: If excessive deposits accumulate over a short time or low mileage, install new valve guide seals to prevent seepage of oil into the combustion chambers. Also try changing gasoline brands.

HIGH SPEED GLAZING

Symptoms: Insulator has yellowish, glazed appearance. Indicates that combustion chamber temperatures have risen suddenly during hard acceleration. Normal deposits melt to form a conductive coating. Causes misfiring at high speeds.
Recommendation: Install new plugs. Consider using a colder plug if driving habits warrant.

OIL DEPOSITS

Symptoms: Oily coating caused by poor oil control. Oil is leaking past worn valve guides or piston rings into the combustion chamber. Causes hard starting, misfiring and hesitation.
Recommendation: Correct the mechanical condition with necessary repairs and install new plugs.

DETONATION

Symptoms: Insulators may be cracked or chipped. Improper gap setting techniques can also result in a fractured insulator tip. Can lead to piston damage.
Recommendation: Make sure the fuel anti-knock values meet engine requirements. Use care when setting the gaps on new plugs. Avoid lugging the engine.

GAP BRIDGING

Symptoms: Combustion deposits lodge between the electrodes. Heavy deposits accumulate and bridge the electrode gap. The plug ceases to fire, resulting in a dead cylinder.
Recommendation: Locate the faulty plug and remove the deposits from between the electrodes.

MECHANICAL DAMAGE

Symptoms: May be caused by a foreign object in the combustion chamber or the piston striking an incorrect reach (too long) plug. Causes a dead cylinder and could result in piston damage.
Recommendation: Repair the mechanical damage. Remove the foreign object from the engine and/or install the correct reach plug.

CONTENTS

QUICK REFERENCE DATA VII

CHAPTER ONE
GENERAL INFORMATION 1

Manual organization   Tools
Service hints   Expendable supplies
Safety first   Mechanic's tips

CHAPTER TWO
PERIODIC MAINTENANCE 8

Engine tune-up   Drive chain
Clutch adjustment   Brakes

CHAPTER THREE
ENGINE, TRANSMISSION, AND CLUTCH 23

Two-stroke operating principles   Engine sprocket
Engine lubrication   Right crankcase cover
Preparation for engine   Clutch
  disassembly   Primary drive gear
Engine removal   Kickstarter
Cylinder and cylinder head   Tachometer drive gear
Piston, pin and rings   Shifter
Reed valve   Crankcase
Flywheel magneto and   Transmission
  starter/generator   Crankshaft

CHAPTER FOUR
CARBURETORS 74

Carburetor operation   Carburetor adjustment
Carburetor overhaul   Miscellaneous problems

CHAPTER FIVE
ELECTRICAL SYSTEM 89

Flywheel magneto operation
Magneto troubleshooting
Capacitor discharge ignition (CDI)
Starter/generator

Lights
Horn
Main switch
Battery

CHAPTER SIX
CHASSIS SERVICE 105

Wheels
Brakes
Front fork

Steering head
Rear suspension
Drive chain

CHAPTER SEVEN
TROUBLESHOOTING 128

Operating requirements
Starting difficulties
Poor idling
Misfiring
Flat spots
Power loss
Overheating
Backfiring

Engine noises
Piston seizure
Excessive vibration
Clutch slip or drag
Poor handling
Brake problems
Lighting problems
Troubleshooting guide

APPENDIX
SPECIFICATIONS 133

INDEX 153

QUICK REFERENCE DATA

MAGNETO IGNITION

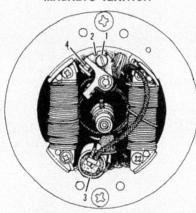

1. Point retaining screw
2. Pry slot
3. Condenser
4. Contacts

BATTERY IGNITION

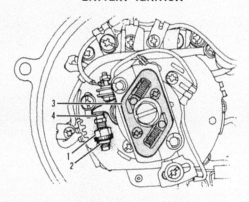

1. Locknut
2. Stationary contact
3. Centrifugal advance
4. Contacts

TUNE-UP SPECIFICATIONS

Breaker point gap	0.012-0.016 in. (0.3-0.4mm)
Ignition timing	
CDI models (YZ100, YZ125, MX175)	Align marks on stator and rotor
Battery ignition models (AT1, AT2, DT125)	0.071 in. (1.8mm)
Magneto ignition models	
(CT series)	0.071 in. (1.8mm)
(all other models except MX)	0.079 in. (2.0mm)
(MX)	0.098 in. (2.5mm)
Spark plug gap	
MX models	0.016-0.020 in. (0.4-0.5mm)
All other models	0.020-0.023 in. (0.5-0.6mm)
Idle speed	
80-100cc models	900-1,000 rpm
125-175cc models	1,000-1,200 rpm

ADJUSTMENTS

Clutch lever free play	0.08-0.12 in. (2-3mm)
Clutch adjustment	See Chapter Two
Rear brake pedal free play	1.0 in. (25mm)
Front brake lever free play	0.20-0.32 in. (5-8mm)
Throttle grip	10° of grip rotation
Autolube pump	See Chapter Two
Drive chain free play	0.75-1.0 in. (20-25mm) total up-and-down movement

TIRE PRESSURE

	Front	Rear
Street use*	24 psi	28 psi
Off-road use**	14 psi	14 psi

*Add 2 psi per tire for sustained high-speed riding and 2 psi to the rear tire if a passenger is carried.

**Use these tire pressures as a guideline only. Experiment with tire pressure to obtain the best traction for the terrain.

FUEL AND LUBRICANTS

Item	Capacity	Type
Autolube	As needed	Special 2-cycle oil
Pre-Mix (YZ125)	15:1 ratio	Special 2-cycle oil
Transmission oil All 80cc models AT2, AT3, CT2, CT3 DT100, DT175, MX100, MX125, YZ125 AT1, AT2-MX, AT-MX, CT1, DT125	0.4 U.S. qt. (0.5 liter) 0.5 U.S. qt. (0.6 liter) 0.6 U.S. qt. (0.65 liter) 0.7 U.S. qt. (0.75 liter)	SAE 10W-30 SE SAE 10W-30 SE SAE 10W-30 SE SAE 10W-30 SE

Front fork legs (each)	1968-1976	1977 and later
YZ80	3.6-3.7 oz. (105-110cc) Lt 3.25 Rt 4.1 oz. (Lt 96 Rt 120cc)	3.8 oz. (112cc) —
YZ125	6.4 oz. (191cc)	6.0 oz. (180cc)
MX100	6.3 oz. (187cc)	—
AT1 series	4.9-5.4 oz. (145-160cc)	—
AT2, AT3 series	4.1 oz. (120cc)	—
DT, MX, YZ125	4.4 oz. (130cc)	5.0 oz. (146cc)
CT1 series	4.9-5.4 oz. (145-160cc)	—
CT2, CT3	4.1 oz. (120cc)	—
DT, MX175	7.1 oz. (210cc)	5.0 oz. (146cc)

Item	Capacity	Type
Drive chain	As needed	SAE 30W or special chain lubricant
Fuel	As needed	86 octane (pump) 91 octane (research)
Fittings, bearings, and bushings	As needed	Lithium grease
Cables	As needed	WD-40 or LPS 25

SPARK PLUGS

	NGK	ND	Autolite
80cc Series	B7HS	W22FS	AE2
AT2, AT3, ST1, CT2, DT125, DT175	B8ES	W24ES	AG901
MX100, YZ125, MX175	B8EV	—	—
AT1	B8E	W24E	AG903
DT100	B8HS	W24FS	AE1
AT1-M	B9E	W27S	A901
AT-MX, AT1-MX, AT2-MX,	B9EN	—	AG603
MX125	B9EV	—	AG603

TIGHTENING TORQUES

Tightening Torques	Ft.-lb.	mkg
Cylinder head nuts		
80cc engines	7.3	(1.0)
All others	14.5	(2.0)
Flywheel nut, rear sprocket nuts	25-29	(3.5-4.0)
Spark plug	18-22	(2.5-3.5)
Engine sprocket and clutch retainer	29-32	(4.0-4.5)
Front and rear axle nuts	29-32	(4.0-4.5)
Swing arm pivot nut	29-32	(4.0-4.5)
Fork cap and stem bolts	25-29	(3.5-4.0)

CHAPTER ONE

GENERAL INFORMATION

This book was written to provide service guidance to owners of Yamaha 2-cycle motorcycles. Its contents apply to all popular 80 cc through 175 cc single cylinder models with dual shock suspensions.

MANUAL ORGANIZATION

Chapters One through Eight and the Appendix give service, repair, and performance improvement information, and specifications for all 1968 through 1976 models.

SERVICE HINTS

The terms NOTE, CAUTION, and WARNING have specific meaning in this book. A NOTE provides additional information to make a step or procedure easier and clearer. Disregarding a NOTE could cause inconvenience, but would not cause damage or personal injury.

A CAUTION emphasizes areas where equipment damage could result. Disregarding a CAUTION could cause permanent mechanical damage; however, personal injury is unlikely.

A WARNING emphasizes areas where personal injury or even death could result from negligence. Mechanical damage may also occur.

WARNINGS are to be taken seriously. In some cases serious injury or death has been caused by mechanics disregarding similar warnings.

Most of the service procedures described in this book are straightforward, and can be performed by anyone who is reasonably handy with tools. It is suggested, however, that you consider your own capabilities carefully before attempting any operation which involves major engine disassembly.

Crankshaft overhaul, for example, requires a press, precision test fixtures, and considerable experience. It would be wiser to have that operation performed by a shop equipped for such work, rather than to try it with makeshift equipment. Other procedures require precision measurements. Unless you have the skills and equipment to make these measurements, call on a competent service outlet.

You will find that repairs will go much faster and easier if your machine is clean before you begin work. There are special cleaners for washing the engine and related parts. You just brush or spray on the cleaning solution, let it stand, and rinse it away with a garden hose. Clean all oily or greasy parts with cleaning solvent as you remove them. *Never use gasoline as a cleaning agent*. Gasoline presents an extreme fire hazard. Be sure to work in a well-ventilated area when you use cleaning solvent. Keep a fire extinguisher handy, just in case.

Special tools are required for some service procedures. These tools may be purchased at Yamaha dealers. If you are on good terms with the dealer's service department, you may be able to use theirs.

Much of the labor charge for repairs made by dealers is for removal and disassembly of other parts to reach the defective one. It is frequently possible for you to do all of this yourself, then take the affected subassembly, such as the crankshaft mentioned earlier, into the dealer for repair.

Once you decide to tackle the job yourself, read the entire section in this manual which pertains to the job. Study the illustrations and the text until you have a good idea of what is involved. If special tools are required, make arrangements to get them before you start the job. It is frustrating to get partly into a job and find that you are unable to complete it.

SAFETY FIRST

Professional mechanics can work for years without sustaining serious injury. If you observe a few rules of common sense and safety, you can also enjoy many safe hours servicing your own machine. You can also hurt yourself or damage the bike if you ignore these rules.

1. Never use gasoline as a cleaning solvent.

2. Never smoke or use a torch near flammable liquids, such as cleaning solvent in open containers.

3. Never smoke or use a torch in an area where batteries are charging. Highly explosive hydrogen gas is formed during the charging process.

4. If welding or brazing is required on the machine, remove the fuel tank to a safe distance, at least 50 feet away.

5. Be sure to use the proper size wrench for turning nuts.

6. If a nut is tight, think for a moment what would happen to your hand should the wrench slip. Be guided accordingly.

7. Keep your work area clean and uncluttered.

8. Wear safety goggles for all operations involving drilling, grinding, or use of a chisel.

9. Never use worn tools.

10. Keep a fire extinguisher handy. Be sure that it is rated for gasoline and electrical fires.

TOOLS

Every motorcyclist should carry a small tool kit with him, to help make minor roadside adjustments and repairs. A suggested kit, available at most dealers, is shown in **Figure 1**.

For more extensive servicing, an assortment of ordinary hand tools is required. As a minimum, have the following available. Note that all threaded fasteners are metric sizes.

    a. Combination wrenches

    b. Socket wrenches

    c. Assorted screwdrivers

    d. Assorted pliers

    e. Spark plug gauge

    f. Spark plug wrench

    g. Small hammer

    h. Plastic and rubber mallets

    i. Parts cleaning brush

A few special tools may also be required. The first four can be considered essential.

1. *Flywheel puller* (**Figure 2**). Yamaha bikes with magnetos require that the flywheel be removed to gain access to the breaker points. This tool costs around $6, and it is available at most motorcycle shops or by mail order from accessory dealers. Be sure to specify the model of your machine when ordering. There is no satisfactory substitute for this tool; but there have been many unhappy owners who bought expensive new crankshafts and flywheels after trying makeshift flywheel removal methods.

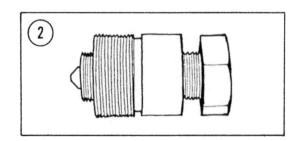

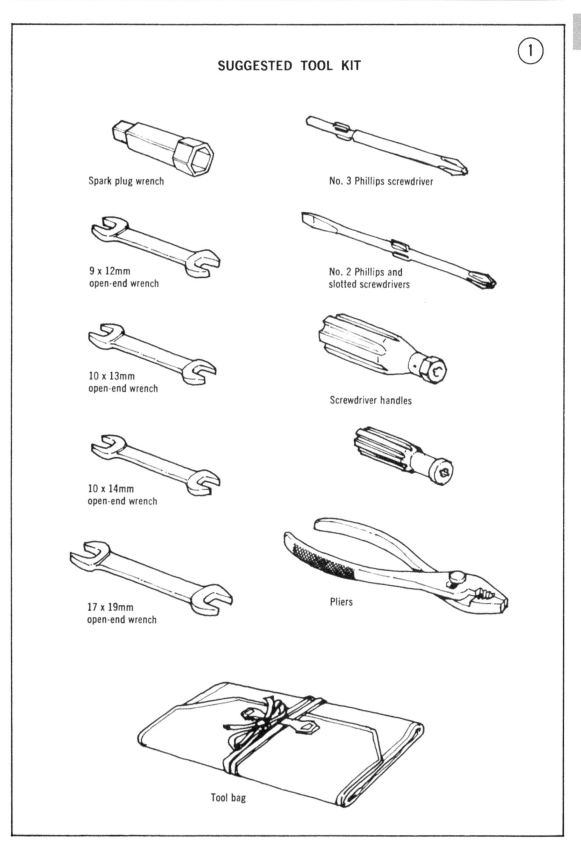

SUGGESTED TOOL KIT

Spark plug wrench

No. 3 Phillips screwdriver

9 x 12mm
open-end wrench

No. 2 Phillips and
slotted screwdrivers

10 x 13mm
open-end wrench

Screwdriver handles

10 x 14mm
open-end wrench

17 x 19mm
open-end wrench

Pliers

Tool bag

2. *Ignition gauge* (**Figure 3**). This tool combines round wire spark plug gauges with narrow breaker point feeler gauges. Most bikes with magnetos require that point gap be adjusted through a narrow slot in the flywheel. Standard feeler gauges will not fit through this slot, making point gap measurement difficult or impossible. This tool costs about $3 at auto accessory stores.

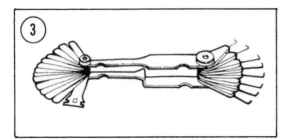

3. *Timing tester* (**Figure 4**). This unit signals the instant when breaker points just open. On models with magnetos, this point is sometimes difficult to determine with a test light or ohmmeter, because the breaker points are shunted by a low-resistance coil.

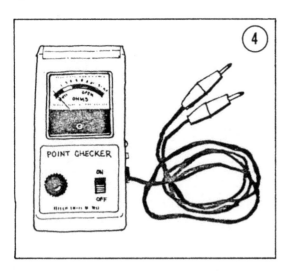

4. *Timing gauge* (**Figure 5**). Yamaha bikes require that ignition timing be set by adjusting the breaker points so that they just begin to open when the piston is at a specified distance below top dead center. By screwing this instrument into the spark plug hole, piston position may be determined.

The tool shown is priced at about $20, and is available from larger dealers and mail order houses. Less expensive ones, which utilize a vernier scale instead of a dial indicator, are also available. They are also satisfactory, but not quite so quick and easy to use.

5. *Hydrometer* (**Figure 6**). This tool measures charge of the battery, and tells much about battery condition. Available at any auto parts store and through most mail order outlets, a typical hydrometer costs less than $3.

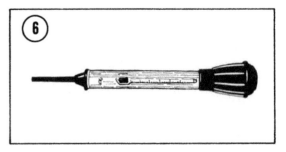

6. *Multimeter, or VOM* (**Figure 7**). This instrument is invaluable for electrical system troubleshooting and service. A few of its functions may be duplicated by locally fabricated substitutes, but for the serious hobbyist, it is a must. Its uses are described in the applicable sections of this book. Prices start at around $10 at electronics hobbyist stores and mail order outlets.

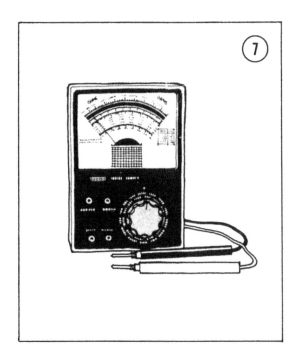

7. *Compression gauge* (**Figure 8**). An engine with low compression cannot be properly tuned and will not develop full power. The compression gauge shown has a flexible stem, which enables it to reach cylinders where there is little clearance between the cylinder head and frame. Less expensive gauges start at around $3, and are available at auto accessory stores or by mail order.

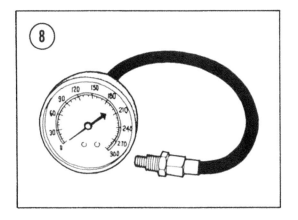

8. *Impact driver* (**Figure 9**). This tool might have been designed with the motorcyclist in mind. It makes removal of engine cover screws easy, and eliminates damaged screw slots. Good ones run about $12 at larger hardware stores.

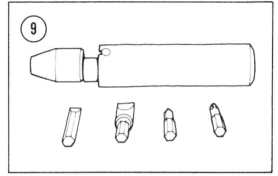

EXPENDABLE SUPPLIES

Certain expendable supplies are also required. These include grease, oil, gasket cement, wiping rags, cleaning solvent, and distilled water. Cleaning solvent is available at many service stations. Distilled water, required for battery service, is available at every supermarket. It is sold for use in steam irons, and is quite inexpensive.

MECHANIC'S TIPS

Removing Frozen Nuts and Screws

When a fastener rusts and cannot be removed, several methods may be used to loosen it. First, apply penetrating oil liberally. Rap the fastener several times with a small hammer; do not hit it hard enough to cause damage.

For frozen screws, apply oil as described, then insert a screwdriver in the slot and rap the top of the screwdriver with a hammer. This loosens the rust so the screw can be removed in the normal way. If the screw head is too chewed up to use a screwdriver, grip the head with vise-type pliers and turn the screw out.

For a frozen bolt or nut, apply penetrating oil, then rap it with a hammer. Turn off with the proper size wrench. If the points are rounded off, grip with vise-type pliers as described for screws.

Stripped Threads

Occasionally, threads are stripped through carelessness or impact damage. Often the threads can be cleaned up by running a tap (for internal threads) or die (for external threads) through the threads. See **Figure 10**.

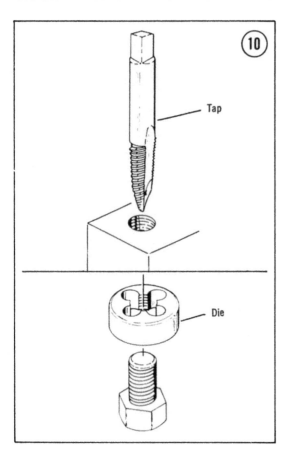

Tap

Die

If the head breaks off flush, as it usually does, remove it with a screw extractor. Refer to **Figure 12**. Center-punch the broken part, then drill a hole into it. Drill sizes are marked on the tool. Tap the extractor into the broken part, then back it out with a wrench.

Removing Frozen Nuts

Nuts subject to corrosion or high temperatures, such as those which retain exhaust pipes, frequently become impossible to remove normally. A nut splitter is an invaluable tool under such circumstances.

To use this tool, merely position it over the offending nut and turn its cutting blade parallel to the stud or bolt from which the nut is to be removed (**Figure 13**). Then turn the pressure screw on the tool until the nut splits (**Figure 14**). Internal forces in the nut will cause it to loosen from the stud so that it may be removed easily. The stud will be undamaged by this procedure.

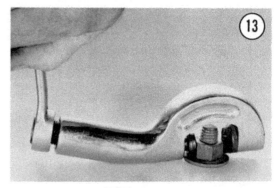

Broken Screw or Bolt

When the head breaks off a screw or bolt, several methods are available for removing the remaining portion.

If a large portion of the remainder projects out, try gripping it with vise-type pliers. If the projecting portion is too small, try filing it to fit a wrench or cut a slot in it to fit a screwdriver. See **Figure 11**.

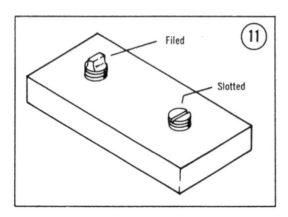

Filed

Slotted

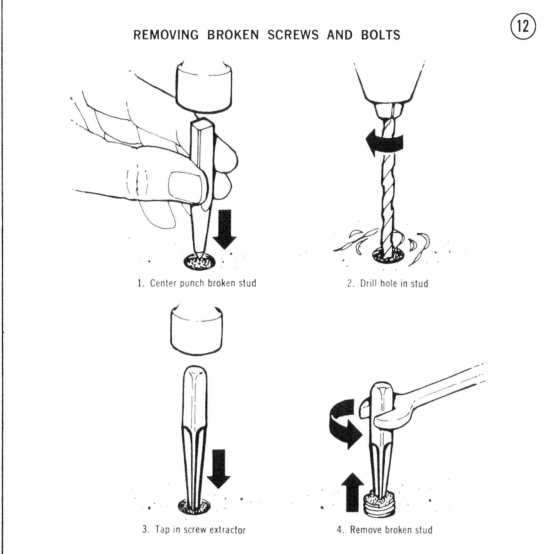

REMOVING BROKEN SCREWS AND BOLTS ⑫

1. Center punch broken stud

2. Drill hole in stud

3. Tap in screw extractor

4. Remove broken stud

CHAPTER TWO

PERIODIC MAINTENANCE

To gain the utmost in safety, performance, and useful life from your motorcycle, it is necessary to make periodic inspections and adjustments. It frequently happens that minor problems found during such inspections are simple and inexpensive to correct at the time, but could lead to major failures later. This chapter describes such services.

Table 1 is a suggested maintenance schedule.

Table 1   MAINTENANCE SCHEDULE

Maintenance Item	Initial 500 Miles	Every 1,000 Miles	Every 2,000 Miles
Check spark plug	x	x	
Engine tune-up			x
Adjust clutch	x	x	
Adjust brakes	x	x	
Check wheels	x	x	
Service chain	x	x	
Check battery	x	x	
Check electrical equipment	x	x	
Tighten all fasteners			x
Clean exhaust system			x

ENGINE TUNE-UP

The number of definitions of the term "tune-up" is probably equal to the number of people defining it. For purposes of this book, we will define a tune-up as a general adjustment and/or maintenance of all service items to ensure continued peak operating efficiency of a motorcycle engine.

As part of a proper tune-up, some service procedures are essential. The following paragraphs discuss details of these procedures. Service operations should be performed in the order specified. Unless otherwise specified, the engine should be thoroughly cool before starting any tune-up service.

Spark Plug

As the first step in any tune-up, remove and examine the spark plug, because spark plug condition can tell much about engine condition and carburetor adjustment.

To remove the spark plug, first clean the area around its base to prevent dirt or other foreign material from entering the cylinder. Then unscrew the spark plug, using a suitable deep socket. If difficulty is encountered removing a spark plug, apply penetrating oil to its base and allow some 20 minutes for the oil to work in. It may also be helpful to rap the cylinder head lightly with a rubber or plastic mallet; this procedure sets up vibrations which help the penetrating oil to work in. Be careful not to break any cooling fins when tapping the cylinder head.

Figure 1 illustrates various conditions which might be encountered upon plug removal.

Normal condition—If plugs have a light tan or gray colored deposit and no abnormal gap wear or erosion, good engine, carburetion, and ignition condition are indicated. The plug in use is of the proper heat range, and may be serviced and returned to use.

Carbon fouled—Soft, dry sooty deposits are evidence of incomplete combustion and can usually be attributed to rich carburetion. The condition is also sometimes caused by weak ignition, retarded ignition timing, or low compression. Such a plug may usually be cleaned and returned to service, but the condition which causes fouling should be corrected.

Oil fouled—This plug exhibits a black insulator tip, damp, oily film over the firing end, and a carbon layer over the entire nose. Electrodes will not be worn. Common causes for this condition are listed below:

   a. Improper fuel/oil mixture
   b. Wrong type of oil
   c. Idle speed too low
   d. Idle mixture too rich
   e. Clogged air filter
   f. Weak ignition
   g. Excessive idling
   h. Autolube pump out of adjustment
   i. Wrong spark plugs (too cold)

Oil fouled spark plugs may be cleaned in a pinch, but it is better to replace them. It is important to correct the cause of fouling before the engine is returned to service.

Gap bridging—Plugs with this condition exhibit gaps shorted out by combustion chamber deposits fused between electrodes. Any of the following may be the cause:

   a. Improper fuel/oil mixture
   b. Clogged exhaust
   c. Autolube pump misadjusted

Be sure to locate and correct the cause of this spark plug condition. Such plugs must be replaced with new ones.

Overheated—Overheated spark plugs exhibit burned electrodes. The insulator tip will be light gray or even chalk white. The most common cause for this condition is use of a spark plug of the wrong heat range (too hot). If it is known that the correct plug is used, other causes are lean fuel mixture, engine overloading or lugging, loose carburetor mounting, or overadvanced ignition timing. Always correct the fault before putting the bike back into service. Such plugs cannot be salvaged; replace them with new ones.

Worn out—Corrosive gases formed by combustion and high voltage sparks have eroded the electrodes. Spark plugs in this condition require more voltage to fire under hard acceleration; often more than the ignition system can supply. Replace them with new plugs of the same heat range.

Preignition—If electrodes are melted, preignition is almost certainly the cause. Check for loose carburetor mounting or overadvanced ignition timing. It is also possible that a plug of the wrong heat range (too hot) is being used. Find the cause of preignition before placing the engine back into service.

Spark plugs may usually be cleaned and regapped, which will restore them to near-new condition. Since the effort involved is considerable, such service may not be worth it, since new spark plugs are relatively inexpensive.

For those who wish to service used plugs, the following procedure is recommended.

1. Clean all oily deposits from the spark plug with cleaning solvent, then blow dry with compressed air. If this precaution is not taken, oily deposits will cause gumming or caking of the sandblast cleaner.

2. Place the spark plug in a sandblast cleaner and blast 3-5 seconds, then turn on air only to remove particles from the plug.

SPARK PLUG CONDITIONS

NORMAL USE

OIL FOULED

CARBON FOULED

OVERHEATED

GAP BRIDGED

SUSTAINED PREIGNITION

WORN OUT

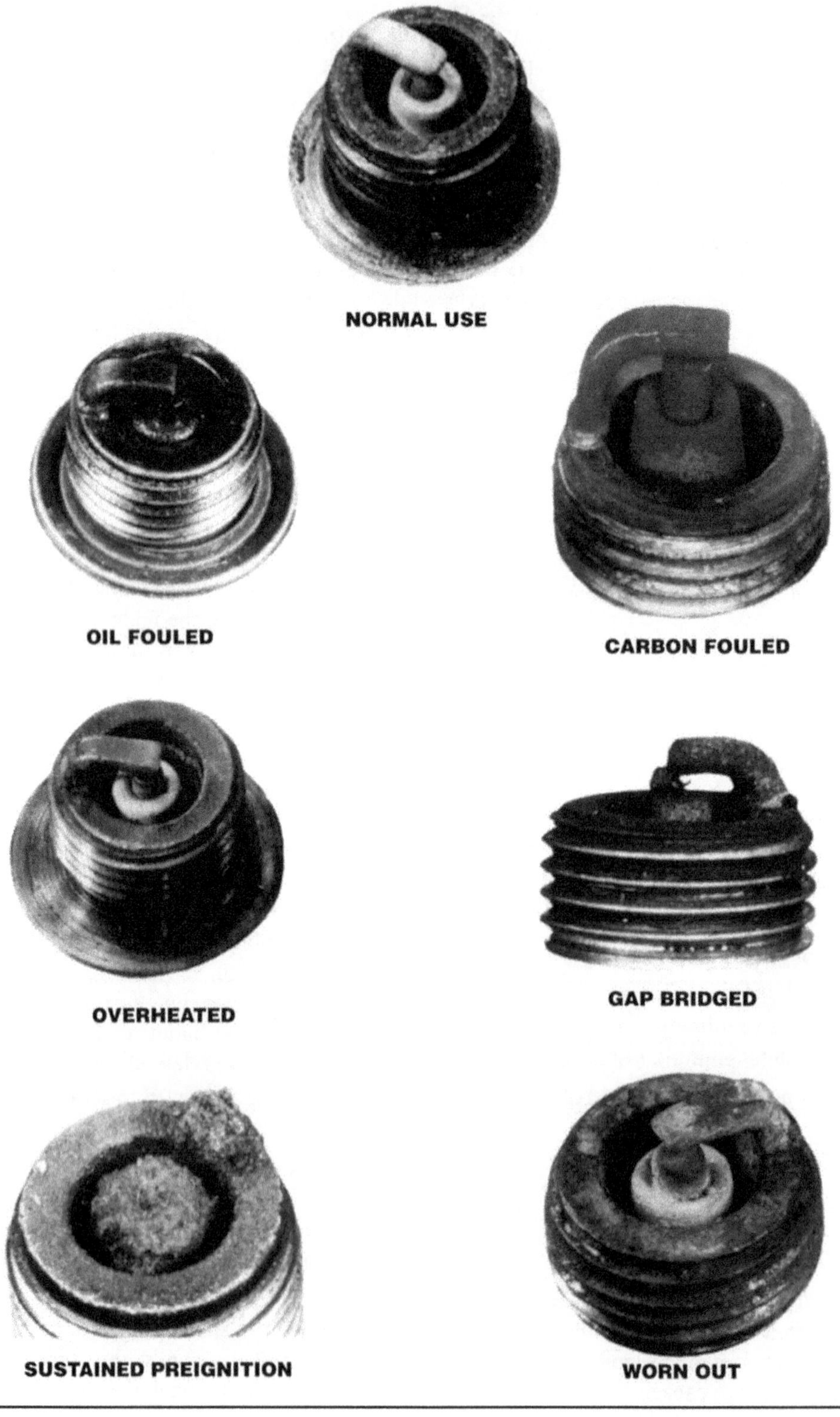

3. Repeat Step 2 as required until the plug is cleaned. Prolonged sandblasting will erode the insulator and make the plug much more susceptible to fouling.

4. Bend the side electrode up slightly, then file the center electrode so that its edges are not rounded. The reason for this step is that less voltage is required to jump between sharp corners than between rounded edges.

5. Adjust spark plug gap to 0.024 in. (0.6mm) for all models. Use a round wire gauge for measurement (**Figure 2**). Always adjust spark plug gap by bending the outer electrode only. A spark plug gapping tool does the best job, if one is available.

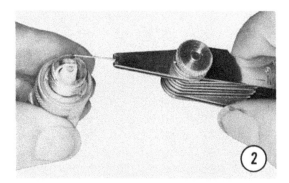

It will be easier to turn the engine over for other service operations if the spark plug is not installed until it is time to start the engine.

Compression Test

An engine requires adequate compression to develop full power. If for any reason compression is low, the engine will not develop full power. A compression test, or even better, a series of them over the life of the bike, will tell much about engine condition.

To make a compression test, proceed as follows.

1. Start the engine, then ride the bike long enough to warm it thoroughly.

2. Remove the spark plug.

3. Screw the compression gauge into the spark plug hole, or if a press-in type gauge is used, hold it firmly in position.

4. With the ignition switch OFF, crank the engine briskly with the kickstarter several times;

the compression gauge indication will increase with each kick. Continue to crank the engine until the gauge shows no more increase, then record the gauge indication.

Example:

1st kick	90 psi
2nd kick	140 psi
3rd kick	160 psi
4th kick	170 psi
5th kick	170 psi

Because of differences in engine design, carbon deposits, and other factors, no definite compression readings can be specified for any one engine. Typical compression pressures will range from 100-150 psi.

A series of measurements made over a period of time may reveal an indication of trouble ahead, long before the engine exhibits serious symptoms. Consider the following example (**Table 2**) for a typical bike. A difference of 20 percent between successive readings over a period of time is an indication of trouble.

Table 2   COMPRESSION HISTORY

Mileage	Compression Pressure (PSI)
New	130
2,000	125
4,000	125
6,000	120
8,000	95

Note that a one-time compression test made at 8,000 miles might be considered normal, but compared with the engine's past history, it is an indication of trouble.

It is for the reasons outlined in the foregoing paragraphs that a serious motorcycle hobbyist will want to own and use his own compression gauge, and also keep a permanent record of its findings. It should be pointed out, however, that measurements taken with different gauges are not necessarily conclusive, because of production tolerances, calibration errors, and other factors.

Carbon Removal

Two-stroke engines are particularly suscep-tible to carbon formation. Deposits form on the inside of the cylinder head, on top of the piston, and within the exhaust port. Combustion chamber deposits can abnormally increase compression ratio, causing overheating, preignition, and possible severe engine damage. Carbon deposits within the exhaust port, exhaust pipe, and muffler restrict engine breathing, causing loss of power.

To remove carbon from the engine, first remove the cylinder head. It is usually unnecessary to remove the piston. Be sure to stuff a clean rag into the crankcase opening to prevent entry of foreign material.

Always allow the engine to cool to avoid possible cylinder head warpage. To remove the cylinder head, proceed as follows.

1. Remove the spark plug.

2. Following a crisscross sequence, loosen each cylinder head retaining nut ¼ turn at a time until each one turns freely. This procedure minimizes chances for cylinder head warpage. Then remove all nuts.

3. Lift the cylinder head from the cylinder (**Figure 3**). If it sticks, tap it lightly with a rubber mallet. Do not pry it off; doing so may cause damage to sealing surfaces.

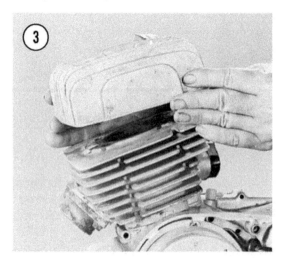

4. Reverse the procedure to install the head. Always use a new cylinder head gasket. Torque cylinder head nuts to 7.5 ft.-lb. (1.0 mkg) on 75cc models, and 15 ft.-lb. (2.0 mkg) on larger models.

An easy method for removing cylinder head deposits is to use the rounded end of a hacksaw blade as a scraper, as shown in **Figure 4**. Be very careful not to cause any damage to the sealing surface.

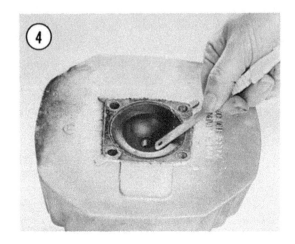

The same tool may be used for removing carbon deposits from piston heads (**Figure 5**). After removing all deposits from the piston head, clean all carbon and gum from the piston ring grooves using a ring groove cleaning tool or broken piston ring (**Figure 6**). Any deposits left in the grooves will cause the piston rings to stick, thereby causing gas blow-by and loss of power.

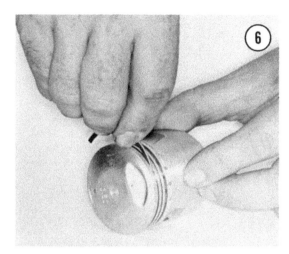

To remove piston rings, it is only necessary to spread the top ring with a thumb on each end (**Figure 7**), then remove it upward. Repeat the procedure for each remaining ring. When replacing rings, be sure that the ends of the rings engage the locating pins in the grooves. See **Figure 8**.

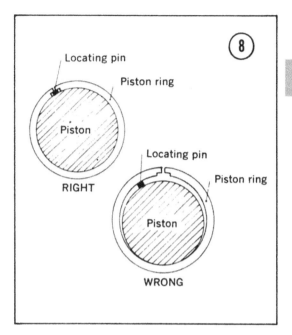

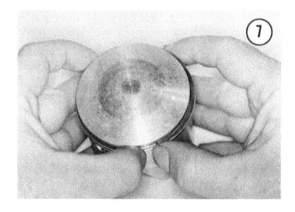

Remove the oil pump output tube at the lower right side of the cylinder. Tap the cylinder lightly at the intake and exhaust ports to loosen it, then lift it from the crankcase (**Figure 9**). Stuff clean rags into the crankcase opening to prevent entry of foreign material.

Scrape all carbon deposits from the cylinder exhaust port, as shown in **Figure 10**. A blunted screwdriver is a suitable tool for this job.

Reverse the removal procedure to install the cylinder. Be sure to lubricate the piston and cylinder liberally before installation. Note that when installing the cylinder, it is necessary to compress each piston ring as it enters the cyl-

inder. A ring compressor tool makes the job easier, but the rings may be compressed by hand with little difficulty.

Breaker Points

Normal use of a motorcycle causes the breaker points to burn and pit gradually. If they are not too pitted, they can be dressed with a few strokes of a clean point file. Do not use emery cloth or sandpaper, because particles can remain on the points and cause arcing and burning. If a few strokes of a file do not smooth the points completely, replace them.

Oil or dirt may get on the points, resulting in poor performance or even premature failure. Common causes for this condition are defective oil seals, improper or excessive breaker cam lubrication, or lack of care when the breaker point cover is removed.

Points should be cleaned and regapped approximately every 1,500-2,000 miles (2,000-3,000 km). To clean the points, first dress them lightly with a clean point file, then remove all residue with lacquer thinner. Close the points on a piece of clean white paper such as a business card. Continue to pull the card through the closed points until no discoloration or residue remains on the card. Finally, rotate the engine and observe the points as they open and close. If they do not meet squarely, replace them.

If poor engine performance has been traced to oil-fouled points, correct the cause before returning the motorcycle to service.

To service or replace breaker points on models with magneto ignition, proceed as follows.

1. Remove gearshift lever. Note that its clamping bolt must be removed completely before the lever can be pulled from the shaft.

2. Remove left crankcase cover. An impact driver makes it easy to loosen the cover screws without damaging them.

3. Remove flywheel retaining nut and its lockwasher.

4. Screw a flywheel puller (left-hand thread) into the flywheel to its full depth. Be sure that the puller screw is backed out fully when installing the puller. Turn the puller screw clockwise to remove the flywheel (**Figure 11**).

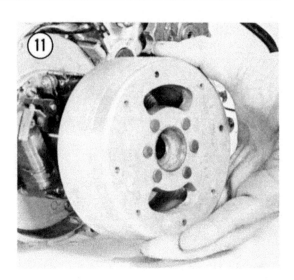

5. Refer to **Figure 12**. Remove the wire, then remove point retaining screw (A).

6. After the new points are installed, tighten screw (A) just enough so that the stationary contact does not slip, but not so much that the contact cannot be moved by a screwdriver twisted in pry slots (B). Move the stationary contact until both points just barely make contact.

7. Install flywheel, lockwasher, and flywheel retaining nut. Tighten flywheel retaining nut securely.

8. Adjust ignition timing.

Breaker point service on models with battery ignition is similar to that on models with magnetos, however point gap must be adjusted separately.

1. Remove ignition cover from left side of engine.

2. Turn engine counterclockwise until breaker points are open to their widest distance apart. Measure point gap (**Figure 13**), using a clean feeler gauge. If point gap is 0.012-0.016 in. (0.30-0.40mm), no adjustment is required.

3. If adjustment is required, refer to **Figure 14**. Using a small wrench, loosen stationary contact locknut, then turn stationary contact until a 0.014 in. (0.35mm) feeler gauge just enters the gap between the fixed and movable points.

4. Tighten locknut, then recheck gap. Readjust if necessary.

5. Adjust ignition timing.

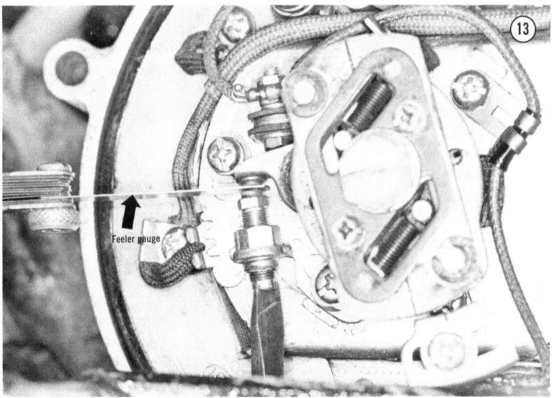

Feeler gauge

1. Locknut   2. Turn stationary contact to adjust gap

Magneto Ignition Timing

1. Using a suitable adapter, mount a dial gauge or other timing tester into the spark plug hole (**Figure 15**). On models with spark plug holes not parallel to the cylinder bore, it is necessary to first remove the cylinder head, and attach the dial gauge to a cylinder stud.

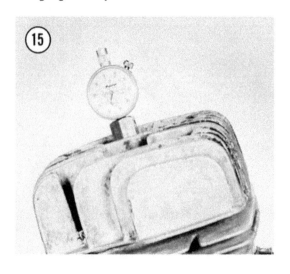

2. Turn engine until dial gauge indicates that piston is at top dead center. Set dial gauge to zero.

3. Turn engine clockwise until piston is about ¼ in. (6mm) below top dead center.

4. Connect a timing tester between the wire on the points and a good engine ground. Follow the manufacturer's instructions for connection.

5. Slowly turn engine counterclockwise until timing tester indicates that breaker points just open.

6. Observe dial gauge. If it indicates the distance specified in **Table 3**, no adjustment is required.

7. If adjustment is required, turn engine until piston is at distance specified in Table 3.

8. Refer to **Figure 16**. Slightly loosen screw (A), then insert a screwdriver into pry slots (B) to move stationary contact until breaker points just open.

9. Tighten screw (A), then recheck and readjust if necessary.

Table 3   MAGNETO IGNITION TIMING

Model	Distance BTDC Inch	(mm)
GT1	0.071	(1.8)
GT80 A	0.071	(1.8)
GTMX, GTMXA	0.071	(1.8)
YX80A	0.071	(1.8)
DT100A	0.071	(1.8)
MX100A	0.079	(2.0)
AT1B-MX, AT1C-MX	0.079	(2.0)
AT1M	0.079	(2.0)
AT2-MX	0.079	(2.0)
ATMX	0.079	(2.0)
MX125A	0.079	(2.0)
CT1, CT1-B, CT1-C	0.071	(1.8)
CT2, CT3	0.071	(1.8)
DT175	0.071	(1.8)

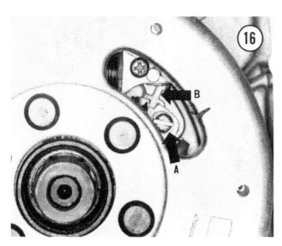

NOTE: *On models so equipped, hold advance lever in full-advance position.*

Battery Ignition Timing

1. Wedge both centrifugal advance weights fully apart (**Figure 17**).

2. Mount a dial gauge in the spark plug hole, using a suitable adapter.

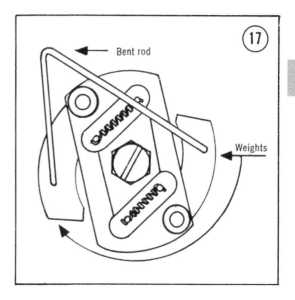

3. Turn engine until the piston is at top dead center, then zero dial gauge.

4. Turn engine clockwise until piston is lowered to distance specified in **Table 4**.

Table 4   BATTERY IGNITION TIMING

Model	Distance BTDC Inch	(mm)
AT2, AT1-B, AT1-C	0.071	(1.8)
AT2, AT3	0.071	(1.8)
DT125A	0.071	(1.8)

Note: Set timing with advance mechanism in Full-advance position.

5. Connect a timing tester between breaker point terminal and a good engine ground. Follow its manufacturer's connection instructions.

6. Refer to **Figure 18**. Slightly loosen both breaker contact mounting plate screws, then using a screwdriver in the pry slots provided, move the mounting plate until the points just open.

7. Tighten both mounting screws, then recheck the adjustment. Readjust if necessary.

CDI Timing

Some models are equipped with electronic ignition (CDI), which uses no breaker points or other moving parts. Once adjusted, ignition tim-

Pry slots

ing should not change, but it should be checked periodically.

1. Remove cylinder head, then mount a dial gauge so that piston position may be determined accurately.

2. Rotate engine counterclockwise until piston is at top dead center. Zero dial gauge.

3. Rotate engine clockwise until piston is at distance below top dead center specified in **Table 5**.

Table 5   CDI TIMING

Model	Distance BTDC Inch	(mm)
YZ100C	0.079	(2.0)
YZ125 A	0.079	(2.0)
MX175A	0.079	(2.0)

4. Refer to **Figure 19**. Mark on rotor must align exactly with long mark on stator. If these marks align, no adjustment is necessary.

5. If adjustment is necessary, refer to **Figure 20**. Loosen both stator plate screws, then turn stator plate as required until marks align.

6. Tighten stator screws.

Air Cleaner Service

As part of any tune-up, air cleaner elements should be cleaned or replaced, as required. A

clogged air cleaner results in an overrich mixture, causing power loss and poor gas mileage. Be sure that the air cleaner element is not torn and that it fits so that no dirt can leak past its edges.

Replace air cleaner elements if they become torn, punctured, or so clogged that dirt cannot be removed.

Some models are equipped with polyurethane foam air cleaner elements. Wash such elements in solvent, dry thoroughly, then wet lightly but

thoroughly wtih engine oil before installation. Replace the element if it is torn or punctured.

Fuel Strainer

Remove and clean the fuel strainer. Blow dry with compressed air. Be sure that the fuel petcock does not leak. Dirty fuel strainers are a major cause of carburetor flooding.

Carburetor Adjustment

Carburetor adjustment is left as the last step to be done on the engine, because it cannot be done accurately until all other adjustments are correct. The carburetor must also be adjusted with the engine thoroughly warmed, while most other adjustments either must be or are more easily done with the engine cold.

Idle speed and idle mixture are normally the only carburetor adjustments performed at the time of engine tune-up. If other adjustments seem to be required, refer to Chapter Four for details of major carburetor service.

1. Turn in idle mixture screw (**Figure 21**) until it seats lightly, then back it out 1¼ turns.

1. Idle mixture   2. Idle speed

2. Start engine, then ride bike long enough to warm it thoroughly.

3. Turn idle speed adjuster until engine runs slower and begins to falter.

4. Turn idle mixture screw as required to make the engine run smoothly.

5. Repeat Steps 3 and 4 to achieve the lowest stable idle speed.

6. Adjust final idle speed as desired.

Autolube Pump Adjustment

1. With engine not running, close throttle (engine idle position).

2. Rotate Autolube pump starter plate (**Figure 22**) in direction of arrow until plunger on forward end of pump moves outward to the end of its stroke.

3. Measure gap between adjustment plate and raised portion of pump pulley (**Figure 23**). This gap should be 0.008-0.010 in. (0.20-0.25mm). Minimum allowable gap is 0.006 in. (0.15mm).

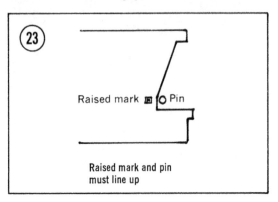

4. If adjustment is required, remove adjustment plate locknut, then adjustment plate. Add or remove shims under adjustment plate as necessary. Adding shims increases gap. Shim stock is available at auto parts stores.

5. Adjust throttle and Autolube pump cables.

Throttle Cable Adjustment

1. See **Figure 24**. With engine idling, loosen locknut on top of carburetor.

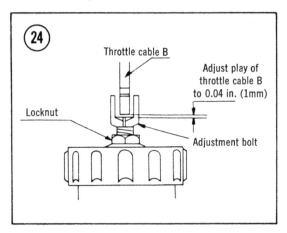

2. Turn adjustment bolt to provide 0.04 in. (1.0mm) slack in throttle cable B.

3. Tighten locknut.

4. Check this adjustment by pulling throttle cable B. Engine speed should not increase until cable has been pulled up about 0.04 in. (1.0mm).

5. Refer to **Figure 25**. Loosen locknut, then turn adjuster to provide 0.02-0.04 in. (0.5-1.0mm) play.

6. Tighten locknut.

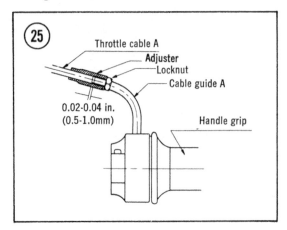

Autolube Cable Adjustment

1. Refer to **Figure 26**. With engine not running, loosen locknut.

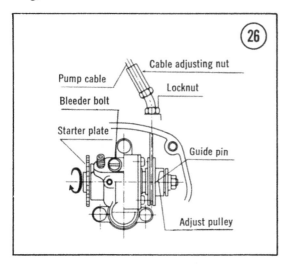

26

Pump cable
Cable adjusting nut
Locknut
Bleeder bolt
Starter plate
Guide pin
Adjust pulley

2. Close throttle fully.

3. Open throttle slowly until all slack in throttle cable is taken up. Hold throttle grip in this position during adjustment procedure.

4. Turn cable adjustment nut until mark on pulley aligns with guide pin.

5. Tighten locknut.

Battery Service

Tune-up time is also battery service time. Complete battery service information is contained in Chapter Five. Briefly, the following items should be attended to regularly.

1. Test state of charge. Recharge if at half charge (1.220 specific gravity) or less.

2. Add distilled water if required.

3. Clean battery top.

4. Clean and tighten terminals.

Oil Change

Probably the single most important maintenance item which contributes to long transmission life is that of regular oil changes. Oil becomes contaminated with products of combustion, condensation, and dirt. Some of these contaminants react with oil, forming acids which attack vital components, and thereby result in premature wear.

To change oil, first ride the bike until it is thoroughly warm. Place a flat pan under the engine, then remove the oil drain plug from the bottom of the engine and allow oil to drain. It may be helpful to rock the motorcycle from side to side and also forward and backward to get out as much as possible.

Replace the drain plug, then refill with fresh engine oil which meets API specification MS or SE. Maintain oil level between both marks on the dipstick.

CLUTCH ADJUSTMENT

Adjust the clutch at 1,000 mile (1,500 kilometer) intervals, or more often if required. Refer to **Figure 27**.

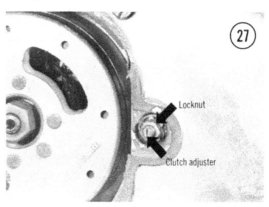

27

Locknut
Clutch adjuster

1. Loosen locknut.

2. Turn adjuster screw in until it seats lightly, then back it out ¼ turn.

3. Tighten locknut. Be sure that adjuster screw does not turn as nut is tightened.

4. Refer to **Figure 28**. Loosen locknut, then turn cable adjuster to obtain about 1/16-1/8 in. (2-3mm) cable slack at clutch lever.

5. Tighten cable adjuster locknut.

ELECTRICAL EQUIPMENT

Check all electrical equipment for proper operation—lights, horn, starter, etc. Refer to Chapter Five for electrical system service.

DRIVE CHAIN

Clean, lubricate, and adjust the drive chain every 1,000 miles (1,500 kilometers), or more

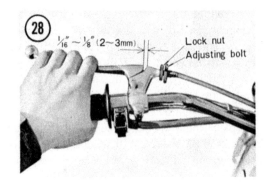

often as needed. Adjust drive chain tension to provide ¾-1 in. (20-25mm) up and down play in the center of the lower chain run. Both wheels should be on the ground and a rider in the saddle when this measurement is made. Be sure to adjust the rear brake after chain tension adjustment.

BRAKES

Adjust front and rear brakes every 1,000 miles (1,500 kilometers), or more often as needed. Remove wheels and check brake lining at 6,000-mile (9,000-kilometer) intervals. Check and service wheel bearings at the same time.

WHEELS AND TIRES

Check wheels for bent rims and loose or missing spokes. Complete wheel inspection and service procedures are detailed in Chapter Six.

STEERING HEAD BEARINGS

Check steering bearings for looseness or binding. *If any exists, find out and correct the cause immediately.* Complete service instructions are in Chapter Six.

CHAPTER THREE

ENGINE, TRANSMISSION, AND CLUTCH

This chapter described removal, disassembly, service, and reassembly of the engine, transmission, and clutch. It is suggested that the engine be serviced without removing it from the chassis except for overhaul of the crankshaft assembly, transmission, or bearings. Operating principles of 2-stroke engines are also discussed in this chapter.

TWO-STROKE OPERATING PRINCIPLES

Figures 1 through 4 illustrate operating principles of piston port engines. During this discussion, assume that the crankshaft is rotating counterclockwise. In Figure 1, as the piston travels downward, scavenging port (A) between the crankcase and the cylinder is uncovered. Exhaust gases leave the cylinder through exhaust port (B), which is also opened by downward movement of the piston. A fresh fuel/air charge, which has previously been compressed slightly, travels from crankcase (C) to the cylinder through scavenging port (A) as the port opens. Since the incoming charge is under pressure, it rushes into the cylinder quickly and helps to expel exhaust gases from the previous cycle.

Figure 2 illustrates the next phase of the cycle. As the crankshaft continues to rotate, the

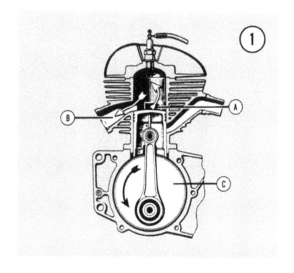

piston moves upward, closing the exhaust and scavenging ports. As the piston continues upward, the air/fuel mixture in the cylinder is compressed. Notice also that a low pressure area is created in the crankcase at the same time. Further upward movement of the piston uncovers intake port (D). A fresh fuel/air charge is then drawn into the crankcase through the intake port because of the low pressure created by the upward piston movement.

The third phase is shown in Figure 3. As the piston approaches top dead center, the spark plug fires, igniting the compressed mixture. The

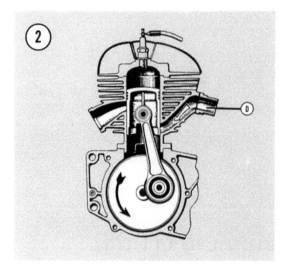

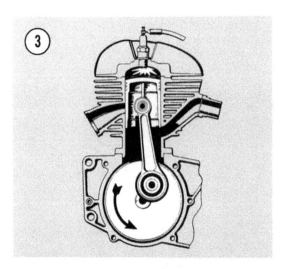

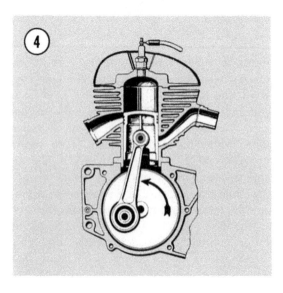

piston is then driven downward by the expanding gases.

When the top of the piston uncovers the exhaust port, the fourth phase begins, as shown in Figure 4. The exhaust gases leave the cylinder through the exhaust port. As the piston continues downward, the intake port is closed and the mixture in the crankcase is compressed in preparation for the next cycle.

For best performance in 2-cycle engines, burned gases from one cycle must be completely expelled from the cylinder, and a maximum charge of fresh fuel/air mixture must be admitted into the cylinder in preparation for the next power stroke.

In conventional engines, if inlet port timing is increased, complete closure of the inlet port will be delayed, and the fuel/air mixture may tend to flow backward through the carburetor. Yamaha's reed valve induction system functions as a one-way valve which prevents reverse fuel mixture flow. The following paragraphs discuss operation of the reed valve.

Figure 5 illustrates system operation as the piston begins to move upward from bottom dead center. The piston begins to close the exhaust port. Fuel/air mixture entering the cylinder forces burned gases out through the exhaust port. As the piston continues upward, crankcase pressure becomes negative, and the holes in the piston skirt uncover the inlet port. Fuel/air mixture then begins to flow into the crankcase through the reed valve and the holes in the piston skirt.

Figure 6 shows the piston as it nears firing position. All cylinder ports are closed, and the combustion chamber is now completely sealed, so the entrapped fuel/air mixture is compressed. The piston skirt has cleared the intake port, so fresh fuel/air mixture continues to be drawn into the crankcase through the open reed valve and intake port.

The spark plug fires and ignites the mixture, driving the piston downward (**Figure 7**). As the piston moves downward, the fuel/air mixture in the crankcase starts to become compressed. Although the holes in the piston skirt open the intake port, the closed reed valve prevents the mixture from backing up through the carburetor.

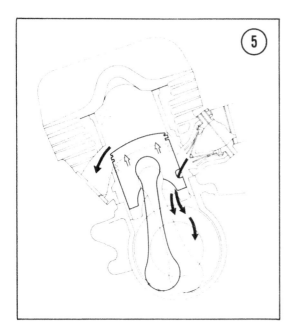

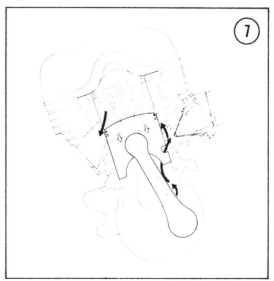

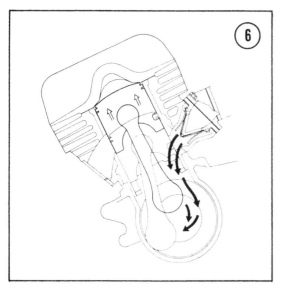

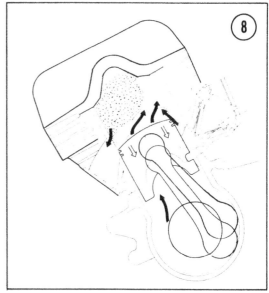

Figure 8 illustrates system operation after the piston has cleared the exhaust port. The mixture in the crankcase has been further compressed. The burned exhaust gases leave the cylinder through the exhaust port. The piston opens the transfer ports shortly after the exhaust port opens. Four streams of fresh fuel/air mixture rush into the cylinder through the transfer ports to help expel residual gases.

Figure 9 illustrates operation of the seventh port. As the piston lowers to the position illustrated, inertia of the exhaust gases leaving the cylinder, plus the incoming fuel/air mixture causes the reed valve to open, and draw more fuel/air mixture directly into the cylinder. This mixture which enters through the seventh port completely bypasses the crankcase.

ENGINE LUBRICATION

It can be seen from the foregoing discussion that the engine cannot receive its lubrication from an oil supply in the crankcase. Oil splash in the crankcase would be carried into the cylinder with the fuel/air charge, resulting in

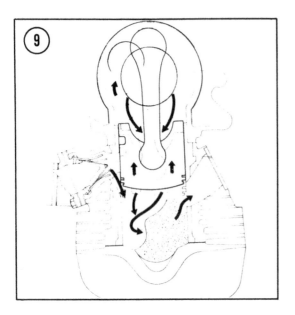

high oil consumption and spark plug fouling. Yamaha 2-stroke engines use one of 2 methods for engine lubrication.

Fuel and Oil Mixture

Some competition models are lubricated by oil premixed with fuel. Sufficient oil is added to the fuel to provide adequate lubrication for the engine under the high speed and load conditions found in competition. Under low speed and load conditions, however, the engine receives more oil than is necessary, resulting in possible plug fouling. In addition, oil starvation can occur in prolonged periods during which the engine turns at high speeds with the throttle closed, as when descending a long hill. These situations don't occur during competition, but could cause problems for machines intended for street use.

Autolube System

To overcome objections to the oil/fuel mixture lubrication method, Yamaha developed its Autolube system. This system is used on most models. A separate engine-driven oil pump supplies oil to the engine induction tract. Oil output from the pump is controlled not only by engine speed, but also by throttle position, which is closely related to engine load. The engine is thereby

supplied with the proper amount of oil under all operating conditions.

Air will enter the Autolube pump whenever the oil supply has run out, or the pump is removed or disconnected. Any air entrapped in the pump or oil lines will result in irregular and inadequate engine lubrication. After such an occurence, the pump must be bled.

To bleed the pump, first remove the bleeder screw shown in **Figure 10**, then rotate the starter plate in the direction of the arrow. Continue to turn the starter plate until no more oil comes out, then replace the bleeder screw. Entrapped air will be bled out more quickly if the throttle is bled fully open as the starter plate is rotated.

Refer to Chapter Two for details of Autolube pump adjustment.

Bleeder screw

In rare situations, wear or a malfunction may result in an autolube pump output that varies from the factory setting (see Chapter Two for pump stroke inspection procedures). If all other troubleshooting efforts fail, you may be faced with a blocked delivery line, or simply a worn out autolube pump. If this is the case, it will have to be corrected immediately, or you may be faced with an expensive engine overhaul job due to damage caused by lack of lubrication.

Removal

1. Remove right crankcase cover.
2. Detach the oil delivery pipe from the cylinder barrel.
3. Unscrew the 2 Phillips head or panhead

screws that hold the pump to the crankcase (**Figure 11**).
4. Disconnect the feeder lines and remove the pump.

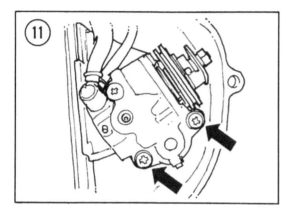

Inspection

1. Inspect the delivery lines that run from the autolube pump to the cylinder and back for possible obstructions.
2. Check all fittings to see if air is being allowed to enter the pump or the engine.
3. Inspect the pump to see if the check ball is missing or improperly installed.
4. Check spring to see if it is worn, missing, or improperly installed.
5. Inspect oil and delivery lines to see if they may have been routed wrong or improperly installed.

Installation

To install the autolube pump, reverse the removal procedures. However, do not install the oil plate covering the autolube pump until you have bled the pump as described earlier.

PREPARATION FOR ENGINE DISASSEMBLY

1. Thoroughly clean the engine exterior of dirt, oil and foreign material, using one of the cleaners formulated for the purpose.
2. Be sure that you have the proper tools for the job. See the general information in Chapter One.
3. As you remove parts from the engine, clean them and place them in trays in the order of their disassembly. Doing so will make

assembly faster and easier, and will ensure correct installation of all engine parts. Keep all related parts together.
4. Note that the disassembly procedures vary slightly between the different models. Be sure to read all steps carefully and follow those which apply to your engine.

ENGINE REMOVAL

The procedure for removing the engine is similar for all models. The following steps are set forth as a guide. Special instructions for individual models are also noted in the procedures.
1. Start the engine and run it a few minutes to warm the transmission oil. Stop the engine and immediately drain the transmission oil. The drain plug is located at the bottom of the transmission case, as shown in **Figure 12**.

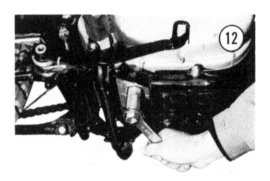

2. Remove the muffler or expansion chamber. On models with through-frame mufflers, detach all retaining hardware, then slide the muffler forward for removal. On models so equipped, unhook both springs at the cylinder, then remove both muffler retaining bolts. On other models, remove the exhaust pipe retaining bolts at the cylinder and those which attach the muffler.

3. Remove the gearshift pedal. It is necessary to completely remove its retaining bolt before the pedal can be pulled from its shaft.

4. Remove the left crankcase cover.

5. Disconnect all wiring from the engine. On models with combination starter/generators, disconnect the wires on the yoke assembly. Don't forget to disconnect the wire at the neutral switch on models so equipped.

6. Remove the master link, then the drive chain. It may be necessary to rotate the rear wheel to position the master link for convenient removal. When installing the chain be sure to position the master link clip as shown in **Figure 13**.

> NOTE: *If the engine sprocket is to be removed, loosen its retaining nut at this time. With the rear brake applied, the drive chain will prevent the sprocket from turning as the nut is loosened.*

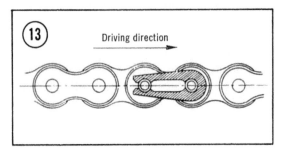

7. Remove the Autolube pump cover (if so equipped), then unwind the cable from the pump pulley and disconnect it. Completely remove the cable adjuster from the engine case.

> NOTE: *After cable installation, operate the throttle to ensure that the cable is wound around the pulley properly.*

8. Disconnect the tachometer drive cable at the lower end, where it screws into the engine case.

9. Disconnect the clamps which secure the rubber boot between the carburetor and air cleaner, then remove the rubber boot.

10. Disconnect the oil line at the tank. Be sure to plug the hole to prevent oil from flowing out.

11. Free the throttle cable from the carburetor. Unscrew the carburetor cap, then pull the slide out to free the cable. Anchor the slide and attached throttle cable out of the way.

> CAUTION
> *When installing the slide, be sure that the cutaway on the lower end of the slide is toward the air cleaner.*

12. Disconnect the fuel line at the fuel petcock. Be sure that the petcock is closed.

13. Disconnect the clutch cable if it is still attached. On most models, it will have been removed with the left crankcase cover.

14. Remove the spark plug cap.

15. Remove all engine mount bolts.

16. Straddle the machine and remove the engine from the frame.

17. Reverse the removal procedure to install the engine. Be sure to check the following items before starting the engine:

    a. Oil supply

    b. Autolube pump adjustment

    c. Clutch adjustment

    d. Oil pump and throttle cables

    e. Drive chain adjustment

    f. Engine mounting bolts

    g. Ignition timing

    h. Transmission oil level (refer to **Table 1**)

Table 1   OIL QUANTITY

Engine Size	Oil Quantity	
(cc)	Fluid Ounces	(Milliliters)
80	15-17	(450-500)
YZ80A	17-19	(500-550)
90	22-25	(650-750)
100	24	(700)
125	24-27	(700-800)
175	24-27	(700-800)

CYLINDER AND CYLINDER HEAD

Cylinder Head Removal/Installation

With the engine cold loosen each cylinder head nut a little bit at a time, in crisscross order, until all are loose. Then remove all nuts. Lift the cylinder head from the cylinder (**Figure 14**). It may be necessary to tap the head lightly with a rubber mallet to free it; if so, take care not to break any cooling fins.

Upon installation, always use a new cylinder head gasket. Torque cylinder head nuts in crisscross order to 14.5 ft.-lb. (2.0 mkg) on all models except those with 80cc engines. Torque nuts on 80cc engines to 7.3 ft.-lb. (1.0 mkg).

Removing Carbon Deposits

Carbon deposits in the combustion chamber cause increased compression ratio and may lead

to preignition, overheating, and excessive fuel consumption. To remove these deposits, scrape them off with the rounded end of a hacksaw blade, as shown in **Figure 15**. Be careful not to damage the gasket surface.

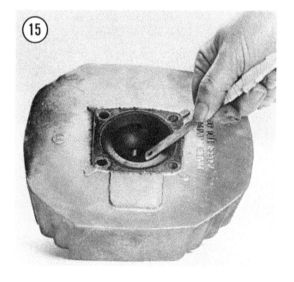

Cylinder Removal

With the cylinder head and oil pump delivery tube (**Figure 16**) removed, tap the cylinder around the exhaust port with a plastic mallet, then pull it away from the crankcase (**Figure 17**). Stuff a clean rag into the crankcase opening to prevent entry of any foreign material.

Checking the Cylinder

Measure cylinder wall wear at locations "a," "b," "c," and "d" with a cylinder gauge or in-

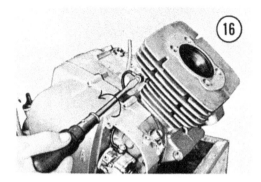

side micrometer, as shown in **Figure 18**. Position the instrument parallel, and then at right angles to the crankshaft at each depth. If the difference between any measurements exceeds 0.0018 in. (0.05mm), rebore them and hone the cylinder to the next oversize, or replace the cylinder. Pistons are available in oversizes of 0.01 in. (0.25mm) and 0.02 in. (0.50mm). After boring and honing, the difference between maximum and minimum diameters must not be greater than 0.0004 in. (0.01mm).

Removing Carbon Deposits

Scrape carbon deposits from around the cylinder exhaust port, as shown in **Figure 19**. The rounded end of a hacksaw blade is a suitable tool for carbon removal.

Cylinder Installation

Be sure that each piston ring and gap is aligned with its locating pin in the ring groove (**Figure 20**). Lubricate the piston and cylinder,

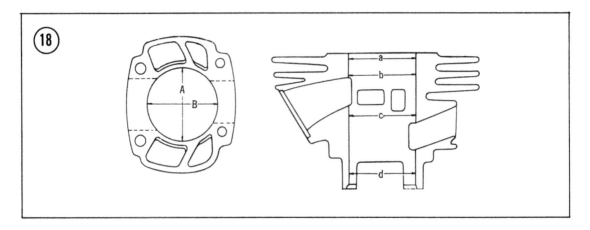

NOTE: *During base gasket installation, make sure the gasket is placed correctly on the crankcase. Check that the gasket matches the irregularly shaped transfer port channels.*

PISTON, PISTON PIN, AND PISTON RINGS

Remove the clip at each end of the piston pin with needle nose pliers (**Figure 21**). Press out the piston pin (**Figure 22**). A tool is available for this job, but it can be done by hand if the piston is first heated by wrapping in rags soaked in hot water.

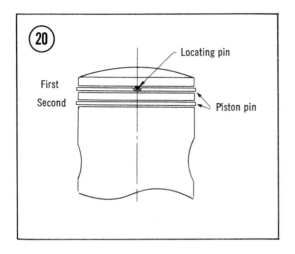

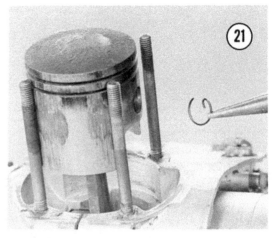

then insert the piston into the lower end of the cylinder. It will be necessary to compress each piston ring as it goes into the cylinder. Always use a new cylinder base gasket upon reassembly, and be sure that all traces of old gasket are removed.

After long service, a ridge may build up around the piston pin clip groove, which makes piston pin removal difficult. In such cases, do not drive the piston pin out by hammering it. Protect the crankcase opening with rags, then carefully chamfer the raised outer groove edge

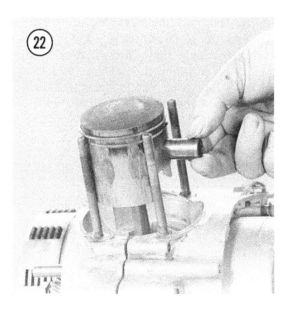

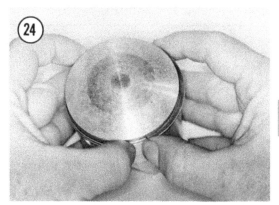

3

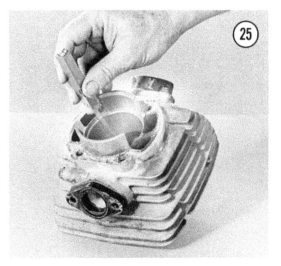

with a knife to scrape away this ridge. The pin should then slide out easily.

Also remove the upper bearing from the connecting rod (**Figure 23**).

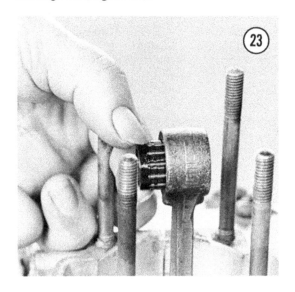

cylinder, then measure ring gap with a feeler gauge. To ensure that the ring is squarely in the cylinder, push it into position with the head of the piston (**Figure 26**). If gap is not as specified in **Table 2**, replace the piston rings.

Piston Rings

Remove the piston rings by spreading the top ring with a thumb on each end, as shown in **Figure 24**. Then remove the ring from the top of the piston. Repeat this procedure for the remaining ring. Some models are equipped with only one ring.

Measure each ring for wear as shown in **Figure 25**. Insert the ring 0.2 in. (5mm) into the

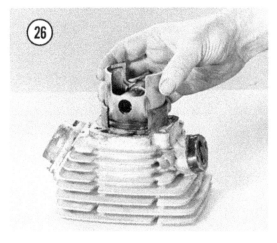

Table 2   PISTON RING GAP

| Engine Size | End Gap | |
(cc)	Inch	(Millimeter)
80-100	0.006-0.014	(0.15-0.33)
125	0.012-0.020	(0.30-0.50)
125 (GYT Kit)	0.016-0.024	(0.40-0.60)
175	0.006-0.014	(0.15-0.40)

Scrape carbon deposits from the head of the piston (**Figure 27**). Then clean all carbon and gum from the piston ring grooves (**Figure 28**) using a broken piston ring, or a ring groove cleaning tool. Any deposits left in the groove will cause the rings to stick, leading to gas blow-by and loss of power.

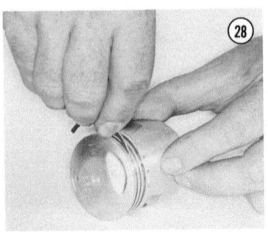

To check fit of the piston ring in its groove, slip the outer surface of the ring into the groove next to the locating pin, then roll the ring completely around the piston (**Figure 29**). If any binding occurs, determine and correct the cause before proceeding. Side clearance tolerances are specified in **Table 3**.

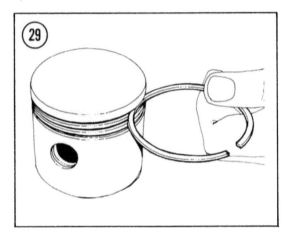

Table 3   PISTON RING SIDE CLEARANCE

| Engine Size | Side Clearance | |
(cc)	Inch	(Millimeter)
80-90	0.0012-0.0028	(0.03-0.07)
100	0.0012-0.0020	(0.03-0.05)
MX100A	0.0012-0.0028	(0.03-0.07)
125	0.0012-0.0020	(0.03-0.05)
MX125A, YZ125A	0.0012-0.0028	(0.03-0.07)
175	0.0012-0.0020	(0.03-0.05)

When replacing rings, install the lower one first. Be sure that any printing on the ring is toward the top of the piston. Spread the rings carefully with your thumbs, just enough to slip them over the piston. Align end gaps with the locating pin in each ring groove.

Some machines are equipped with Keystone pistons and rings. Keystone and conventional rings are compared in **Figures 30 and 31**. The design of the Keystone ring uses combustion gas pressure to force the ring outward against the cylinder wall (**Figure 32**).

An important advantage of the Keystone ring is illustrated in **Figure 33**. As the piston moves up and down, the piston ring tends to move in-

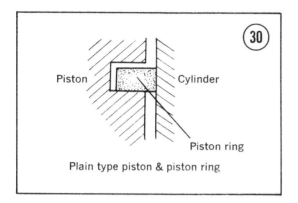

Plain type piston & piston ring

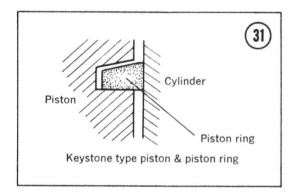

Keystone type piston & piston ring

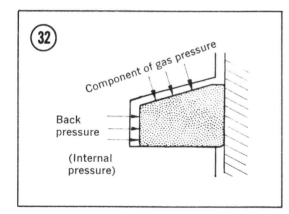

(Internal pressure)

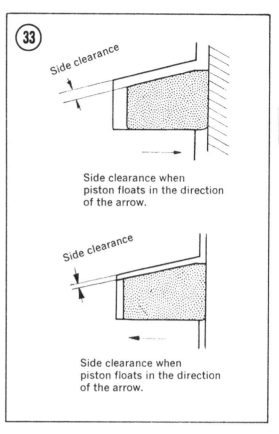

Side clearance when piston floats in the direction of the arrow.

Side clearance when piston floats in the direction of the arrow.

ward and outward, thus varying ring land clearance. This varying clearance tends to prevent the ring from sticking in its groove.

The outer surface of the Keystone ring is Teflon coated. This Teflon coating aids ring seating. Also, the coating tends to follow microscopic irregularities in the cylinder, thereby reducing blow-by.

Keystone rings can be identified by their shape; the top and bottom edges are not parallel. Keystone rings are not interchangeable with the conventional type, and must be used with Keystone pistons. Keystone pistons may be identified by the "K" stamped on the crown after the piston size. Keystone rings are handled in the same manner as conventional rings.

Piston Reconditioning

A piston exhibiting signs of seizure will result in noise, loss of power, and damage to the cylinder wall. If such a piston is reused without correction, another seizure will develop. To correct this condition, lightly smooth the affected area with No. 400 emery paper or a fine oilstone (**Figure 34**).

Replace the piston if the seizure marks cannot be removed with absolute minimal polishing. If in any doubt, replace the piston.

Carefully examine the entire piston surface. Check for cracks, partially melted piston crown, score marks, broken or deformed ring grooves, or any other damage that might interfere with correct piston performance. Replace the piston if any of these defects are noticed.

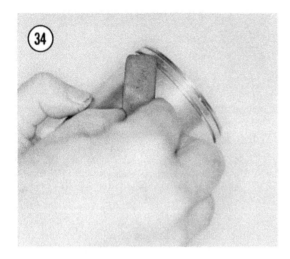

Table 4   PISTON CLEARANCE

| Engine Size | Clearance | |
(cc)	Inch	(Millimeter)
80	0.0014-0.0016	(0.035-0.040)
90	0.0016-0.0018	(0.040-0.045)
100	0.0016-0.0018	(0.040-0.045)
125 (enduros)	0.0016-0.0018	(0.040-0.045)
125 (MX)	0.0016-0.0020	(0.040-0.050)
125 (YZ)	0.0018-0.0020	(0.045-0.050)
175	0.0016-0.0018	(0.040-0.045)

Checking and Correcting Piston Clearance

Piston clearance is the difference between maximum piston diameter and minimum cylinder diameter. Measure outside diameter of the piston skirt (**Figure 35**) at right angles to the piston pin. The measurement should be made 0.02 in. (5mm) from the bottom of the piston. Proper piston clearances are listed in **Table 4**. Any clearance greater than 0.004 in. (0.10mm) will result in noise, in which case necessary repairs should be made.

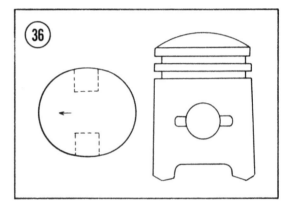

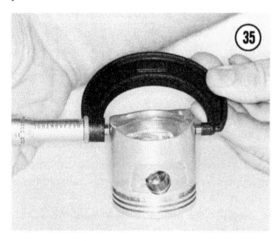

Piston Installation

Install the piston with the arrow mark (**Figure 36**) pointing toward the front of the machine. This step is vital because the hole for the piston pin is offset slightly to prevent piston slap.

Piston Pin

The piston pin should fit snugly in its bore in the piston so that it drags slightly as you turn it. If the piston pin is loose, replace the pin and/or the piston. If the pin shows step wear in the center, replace the needle bearing in the upper end of the connecting rod as well as the piston pin. Check the small end of the connecting rod for wear by assembling the piston pin and upper end bearing (**Figure 37**).

REED VALVE

Reed valve service is similar for all models so equipped. Pay particular attention to the instructions regarding handling of the assembly.

CAUTION
The reed valve is a precision component, and it must be handled with great care. Store the assembly in a clean, dry place, and do not expose it to sunlight. Take special care not to touch its working parts with your fingers.

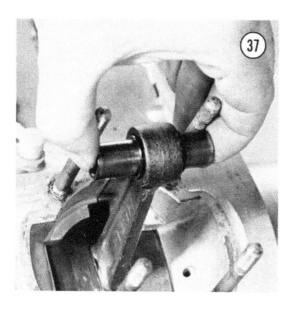

Figure 38 illustrates reed valve construction. Stainless steel reeds (a) open and close the inlet port in response to crankcase pressure changes.

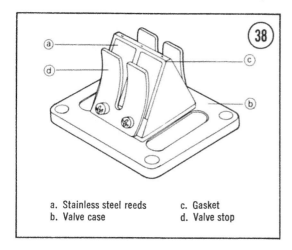

a. Stainless steel reeds
b. Valve case
c. Gasket
d. Valve stop

Removal and Installation

1. Remove carburetor.

2. Remove valve assembly.

3. Reverse the removal procedure to install the reed valve assembly.

Maintenance

Reed valve maintenance is limited to inspection of components and tightening of loose screws. Check for cracks or breakage. Be sure that the bond between the gasket and valve case is not broken. Tighten the screws to 7 in.-lb. (8.0

cmkg). Replace the entire assembly if any component is defective.

FLYWHEEL MAGNETO AND STARTER/GENERATOR

Removal and installation only of these components is discussed in this chapter. Refer to Chapter Five for troubleshooting, or to Chapter Two for routine service.

Magneto Removal and Installation

Magneto removal is similar for all models.

CAUTION
Do not attempt to remove the flywheel unless a suitable puller is available.

1. Remove flywheel retaining nut, flat washer, and lockwasher. A flywheel retaining tool is available to hold the flywheel while its retaining nut is loosened. If this tool is not available, a strap wrench works well. Another method is to feed a rolled-up rag between the primary reduction gears on the other side of the engine to prevent the engine from turning.

2. Screw a flywheel puller (left-hand thread) to its full depth into the flywheel center hole. Be sure that the puller screw is backed out fully before attaching the puller.

3. Turn the puller screw clockwise to remove the flywheel (**Figure 39**).

4. Remove the stator plate (**Figure 40**) after taking out its retaining screws.

5. Remove the Woodruff key from the crankshaft. To prevent this key from becoming lost,

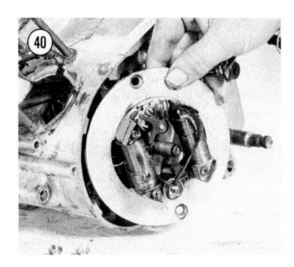

1. Brush in position for installation
2. Brush in normal position

place it on one of the magnets inside the flywheel.

Reverse the foregoing procedure to install
the magneto. Apply a very thin coating of distributor cam lubricant to the breaker cam inside
the flywheel before installation. Be sure that the
Woodruff key is in place.

CAUTION
*Before installing the flywheel, be sure
that no particles adhere to the magnets.*

**Starter/Generator Removal
and Installation**

1. Remove the armature retaining bolt, then
pull off the breaker cam and ignition advance
mechanism.
2. Remove both yoke mounting screws.
3. Pull yoke from engine.
4. Using a suitable puller, remove armature.
5. Remove the Woodruff key from the crankshaft.

Reverse the removal procedure to install the
starter/generator. It is much easier to install the
yoke if all brushes are held up by their springs
(**Figure 41**) until the mounting screws are in
place. Don't forget to snap brush springs back
into position.

ENGINE SPROCKET
Removal

1. Use a blunted chisel to straighten the tab on
the lockwasher.

2. Remove retaining nut, then pull off the
sprocket (**Figure 42**).

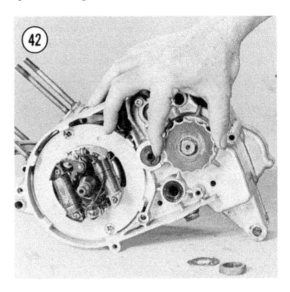

3. Using a pair of pliers, remove the sprocket
spacer.

Inspection

Inspect sprocket teeth for wear. Excessive
wear results in shortened drive chain life. Replace the sprocket if it is worn. **Figure 43** com-
pares worn and serviceable sprockets.

Installation

Reverse the removal procedure to install the
sprocket. Be sure to apply grease to the oil seal
lip. Don't forget to bend up on edge of the
lockwasher.

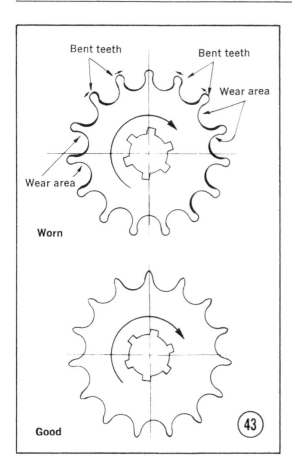

Bent teeth

Bent teeth

Wear area

Wear area

Worn

Good

(43)

2. Remove oil delivery line at cylinder.

3. Remove all cover retaining screws. Don't forget the screw under the Autolube pump cover.

4. Rap cover with a rubber mallet if necessary, then pull it from engine.

Reverse the removal procedure to install the cover. Always install a new cover gasket. Replace the kickstarter oil seal if it leaks, or if its condition is doubtful.

CLUTCH

All models are equipped with wet multidisc clutches. Service on all clutches is similar; differences are pointed out where they exist. **Table 5** lists the various types of clutches. **Figures 44 through 47** are exploded views of each type of clutch. Refer to the applicable illustration during disassembly.

NOTE: *When disassembling clutch, pay particular attention to the way that all small parts, such as spacers and thrust washers, are installed.*

Table 5   CLUTCH TYPE

Model	Type	Figure
GT1	1	44
GTMX	1	44
GT80A	1	44
GTMXA	1	44
YZ80A	1	44
DT100A	2	45
MX100A	2	45
YZ100C	2	45
YZ125A	2	45
DT175A	2	45
AT2	3	46
AT3	3	46
DT125	3	46
AT1	4	47
CT1	4	47

RIGHT CRANKCASE COVER

It is necessary to remove the right crankcase cover to gain access to the primary reduction gears, clutch, shifter, and kickstarter. It is not necessary to remove the Autolube pump to remove the cover.

NOTE: *There is a small quantity of oil under the cover. Place a suitable drain pan underneath before removing the cover. Also be sure to check and replenish the transmission oil upon installation.*

To remove the cover, proceed as follows:

1. Remove pinch bolt from kickstarter lever, then pull kickstarter lever from its shaft.

NOTE: *YZ models require brake pedal and right foot peg removal prior to case cover removal. Also, these machines are not equipped with Autolube; disregard any reference to that system for these machines.*

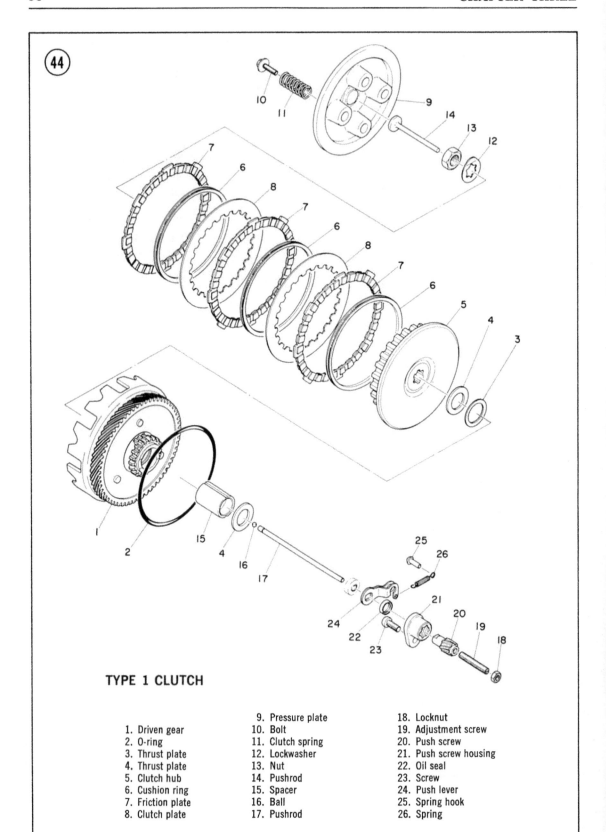

TYPE 1 CLUTCH

1. Driven gear
2. O-ring
3. Thrust plate
4. Thrust plate
5. Clutch hub
6. Cushion ring
7. Friction plate
8. Clutch plate
9. Pressure plate
10. Bolt
11. Clutch spring
12. Lockwasher
13. Nut
14. Pushrod
15. Spacer
16. Ball
17. Pushrod
18. Locknut
19. Adjustment screw
20. Push screw
21. Push screw housing
22. Oil seal
23. Screw
24. Push lever
25. Spring hook
26. Spring

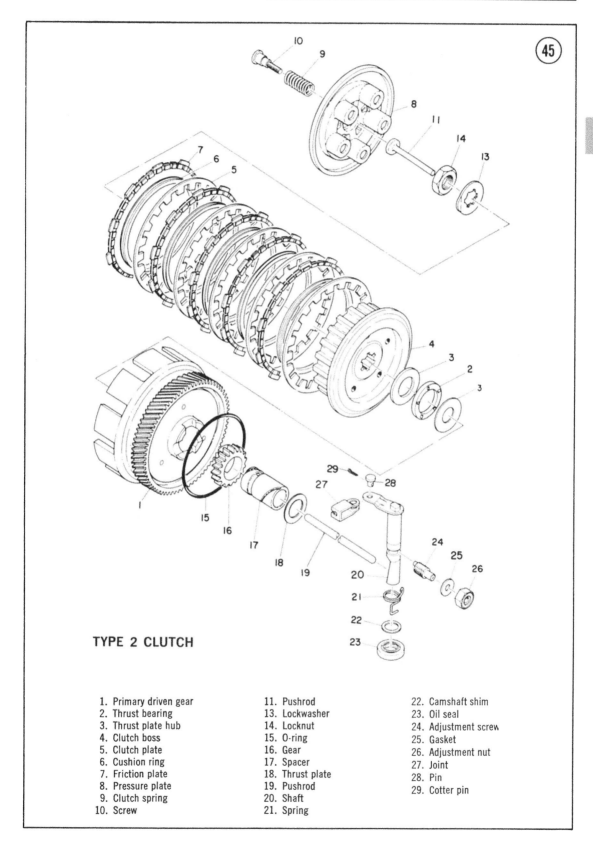

TYPE 2 CLUTCH

1. Primary driven gear	11. Pushrod	22. Camshaft shim
2. Thrust bearing	13. Lockwasher	23. Oil seal
3. Thrust plate hub	14. Locknut	24. Adjustment screw
4. Clutch boss	15. O-ring	25. Gasket
5. Clutch plate	16. Gear	26. Adjustment nut
6. Cushion ring	17. Spacer	27. Joint
7. Friction plate	18. Thrust plate	28. Pin
8. Pressure plate	19. Pushrod	29. Cotter pin
9. Clutch spring	20. Shaft	
10. Screw	21. Spring	

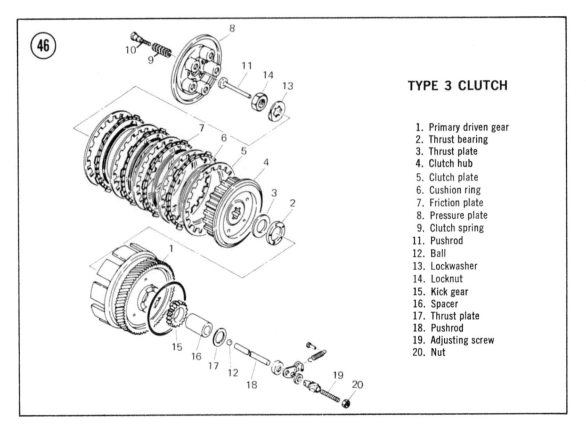

TYPE 3 CLUTCH

1. Primary driven gear
2. Thrust bearing
3. Thrust plate
4. Clutch hub
5. Clutch plate
6. Cushion ring
7. Friction plate
8. Pressure plate
9. Clutch spring
11. Pushrod
12. Ball
13. Lockwasher
14. Locknut
15. Kick gear
16. Spacer
17. Thrust plate
18. Pushrod
19. Adjusting screw
20. Nut

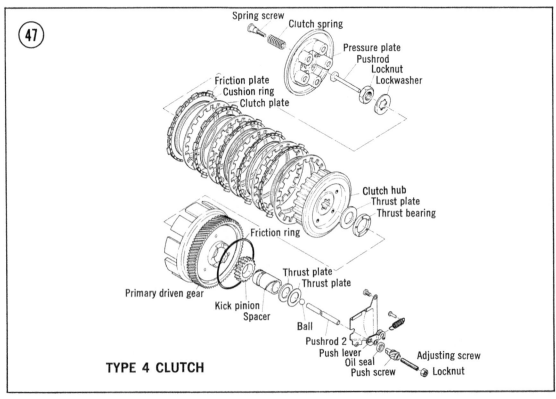

TYPE 4 CLUTCH

Disassembly

1. Remove all clutch springs, then pull out pressure plate (**Figure 48**).

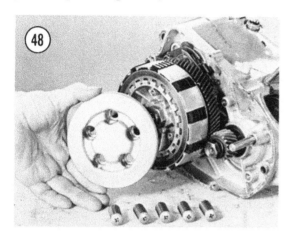

2. Remove clutch hub retaining nut and lockwasher (**Figure 49**).

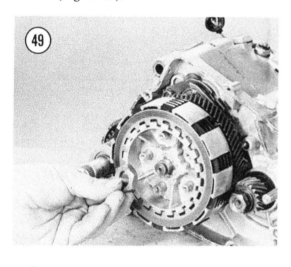

An easy way to fabricate a clutch holder is to weld a short handle to a discarded clutch plate. Another way to hold the clutch is to loop a fan belt of suitable length around the clutch, then secure its other end to the motorcycle frame.

3. Remove pushrod (**Figure 50**). There is a small steel ball behind this pushrod. Tip the engine to the right to remove it, or use a small magnet. Pull out long pushrod, if necessary, from left side of engine.

4. Pull out all metal plates, fiber plates, and rubber rings (**Figure 51**).

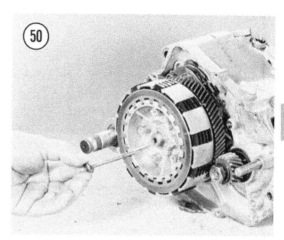

5. Remove clutch hub (**Figure 52**).

6. Remove thrust washers and flat thrust bearing, if so equipped (**Figure 53**).

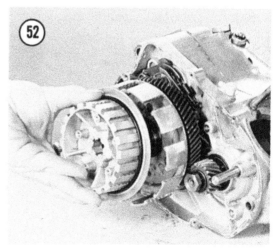

7. Slide clutch housing from transmission input shaft (**Figure 54**).

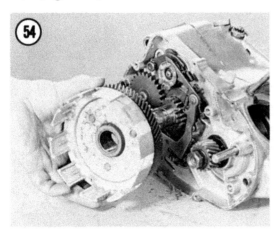

8. Remove spacer and kickstarter gear (**Figure 55**). Note carefully how these parts are installed.

9. Remove spacer next to transmission bearing.

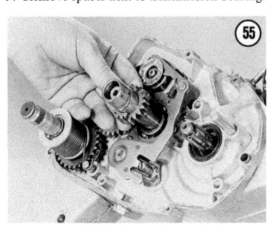

Inspection

Measure free length of each clutch spring (**Figure 56**). If any spring is shorter by 0.04 in. (1.0mm) than the standard length specified in **Table 6**, replace all springs as a set.

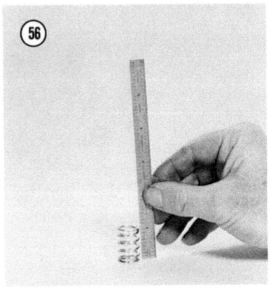

Table 6   CLUTCH SPRING LENGTH

Engine Size (cc)	Inches	(Millimeters)
80	1.24	(31.5)
90	1.34	(34.0)
100	1.34	(34.0)
125 (to 1973)	1.24	(31.5)
125 (1974 on)	1.34	(34.0)
175 (to 1973)	1.24	(31.5)
175 (1974 on)	1.34	(34.0)

Measure thickness of each friction disc at several places (**Figure 57**). Replace any disc that is worn unevenly, or to the limits specified in **Table 7**.

Check each metal plate for warpage by placing it on a surface plate. Then try to insert a 0.004 in. (0.10mm) feeler gauge between the clutch plate and surface plate, from both the outside and inside. If the feeler gauge slips between them, replace the clutch plate.

On some models, there is a rubber ring between the clutch housing and primary driven

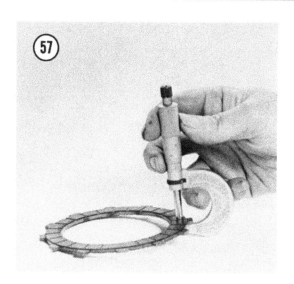

Table 7 CLUTCH PLATE SPECIFICATIONS

Engine Size (cc)	Plate Thickness Inch	(mm)	Wear Limit Inch	(mm)
80	0.138	(3.5)	0.014	(0.35)
YZ80A	0.138	(3.5)	0.012	(0.30)
90-175	0.157	(4.0)	0.016	(0.40)

gear. This ring reduces gear noise at low engine speeds. Be sure that it is in good condition.

Be sure that the slots in the clutch hub and clutch housing are in good condition (**Figure 58**). If deep notches exist, they can hinder clutch disengagement.

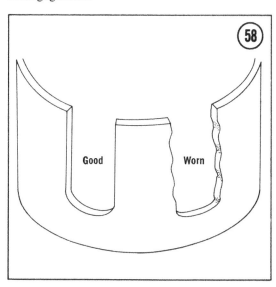

Good   Worn

Insert the primary gear spacer into the clutch housing bearing (**Figure 59**), then check for radial play. If play is excessive, replace the spacer. Allowable clearance is 0.004-0.0017 in. (0.01-0.048mm). Replace the spacer if it is scratched.

Check the gear teeth on the clutch housing for burrs, nicks, or other damage. Smooth any such defects with an oilstone. If the oilstone doesn't smooth out the damage, replace the clutch housing.

Remove all oil from the primary gear spacer and transmission main shaft. Then slide the spacer over the shaft (**Figure 60**) and measure clearance between them. Replace the spacer if radial clearance is not 0.008-0.0024 in. (0.020-0.062mm), or if the spacer exhibits step wear.

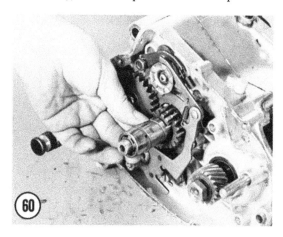

Remove the pushrod and check it for straightness by rolling it on a surface known to be flat. If the rod is bent, straighten or replace it.

Installation

1. Be sure that all thrust washers, plates, and bearings are in proper position.

2. Make sure both kick pinion gear protruding dogs engage the 2 squared-off slots in the back of the primary driven gear. Take care, there are also 2 rounded slots that the dogs could accidentally engage.

3. After installing the primary driven gear assembly, slide on the thrust washers, then carefully slide on the clutch hub. Take care, pulling the clutch hub out after it has been installed could easily dislodge the thrust washers and prevent the hub from sliding in completely.

4. Slide in alternate metal and fiber plates. If your machine has rubber cushions, install one over the clutch hub after each metal plate. The open end faces out. Make sure they are not twisted. These cushions help separate the plates during disengagement. They are helpful, but not required for clutch operation.

> NOTE: *If your model has an extra thick metal clutch plate, install this first onto the clutch hub, before any other plate.*

5. Install the long pushrod, ball bearing, and short pushrod into the transmission shaft hole.

6. Add the pressure plate, springs, and spring retaining screws. Tighten the spring retaining screws just until slightly snug. Excessive torque can snap the screw, which will require clutch hub replacement.

PRIMARY DRIVE GEAR

To remove the primary drive gear, feed a rolled-up rag between the primary drive and primary driven gears to lock them. Consider the direction the gears tend to turn as you loosen the locknut, then pull the gear from the crankshaft (**Figure 61**). If the gear does not come off easily, pry it off with a pair of heavy screwdrivers.

> NOTE: *Always place rags or wood blocks between case and pry tools to prevent gasket surface damage.*

After primary drive gear removal, an O-ring will be visible in a groove on the crankshaft. Make sure this O-ring is installed before primary drive gear installation. Failure to install it will result in fouled plugs and visible exhaust smoke because of transmission oil seeping past where the O-ring should be sealing. Replace this seal if it is flattened or nicked.

Always lubricate the crankshaft seal lips so the primary drive gear will slide through without tearing this seal.

KICKSTARTER

There are 4 basic types of kickstarter mechanisms on Yamaha models covered by this book. **Table 8** lists kickstarter types installed on various models. **Figures 62 through 65** are exploded views of those mechanisms. Refer to the applicable illustration during disassembly, service and reassembly.

Table 8   KICKSTARTER TYPES

Model	Type	Figure
GT series	1	62
AT series	2	63
CT series	2	63
DT100A	3	64
MX100	3	64
DT125A	3	64
MX125A	3	64
DT175A	3	64
YZ125A	4	65

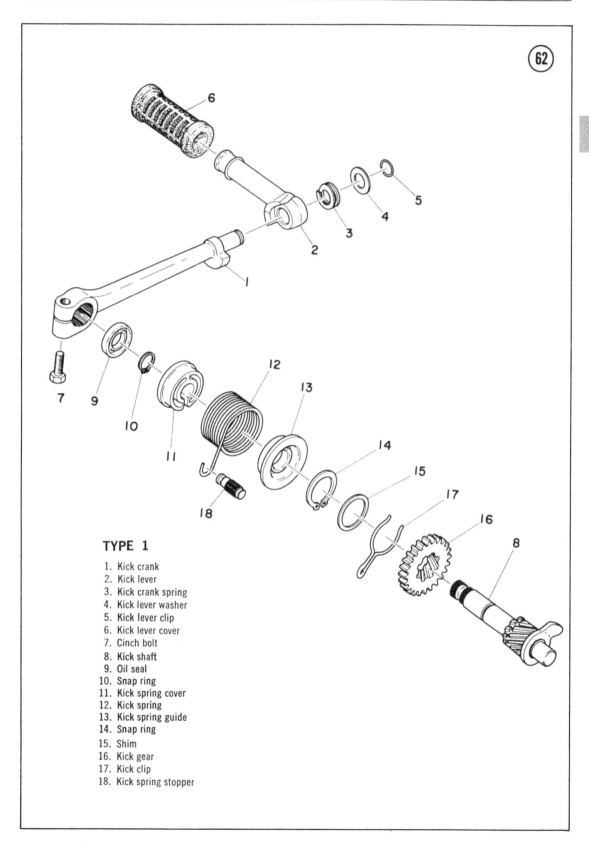

TYPE 1

1. Kick crank
2. Kick lever
3. Kick crank spring
4. Kick lever washer
5. Kick lever clip
6. Kick lever cover
7. Cinch bolt
8. Kick shaft
9. Oil seal
10. Snap ring
11. Kick spring cover
12. Kick spring
13. Kick spring guide
14. Snap ring
15. Shim
16. Kick gear
17. Kick clip
18. Kick spring stopper

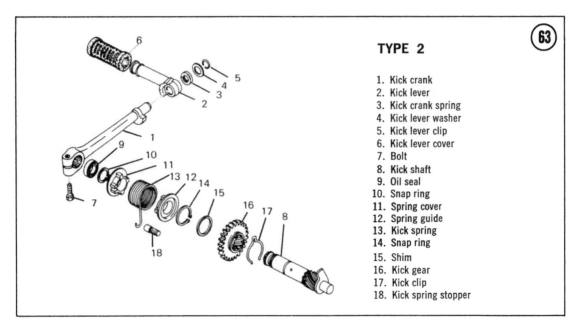

TYPE 2 ⑥③

1. Kick crank
2. Kick lever
3. Kick crank spring
4. Kick lever washer
5. Kick lever clip
6. Kick lever cover
7. Bolt
8. Kick shaft
9. Oil seal
10. Snap ring
11. Spring cover
12. Spring guide
13. Kick spring
14. Snap ring
15. Shim
16. Kick gear
17. Kick clip
18. Kick spring stopper

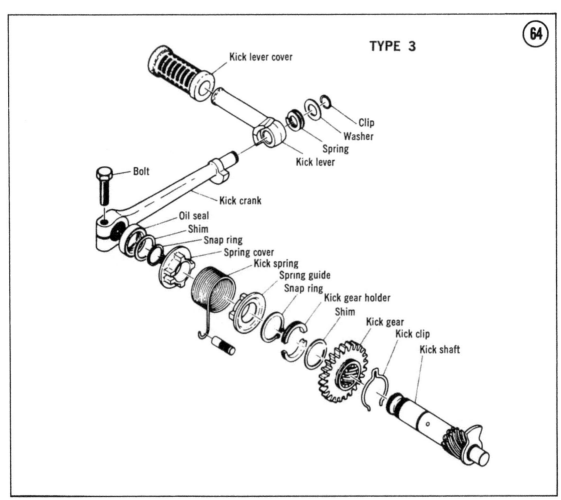

TYPE 3 ⑥④

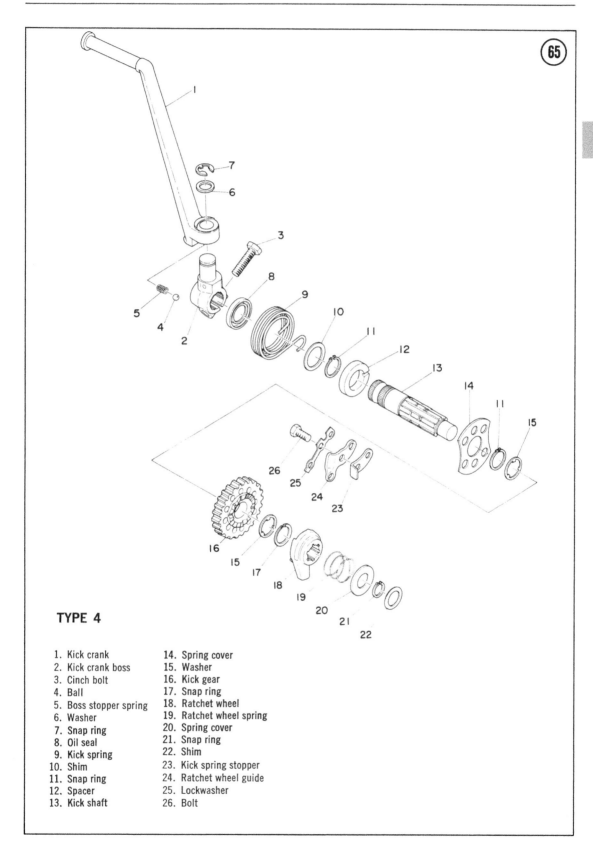

TYPE 4

1. Kick crank
2. Kick crank boss
3. Cinch bolt
4. Ball
5. Boss stopper spring
6. Washer
7. Snap ring
8. Oil seal
9. Kick spring
10. Shim
11. Snap ring
12. Spacer
13. Kick shaft
14. Spring cover
15. Washer
16. Kick gear
17. Snap ring
18. Ratchet wheel
19. Ratchet wheel spring
20. Spring cover
21. Snap ring
22. Shim
23. Kick spring stopper
24. Ratchet wheel guide
25. Lockwasher
26. Bolt

Removal

Kickstarter removal is generally similar for all models.

1. Unhook kickstarter spring (**Figure 66**). Be careful, this spring is under considerable tension.

2. Rotate kickstarter shaft about 45 degrees counterclockwise to free it from the ratchet wheel guide, then pull it straight out (**Figure 67**).

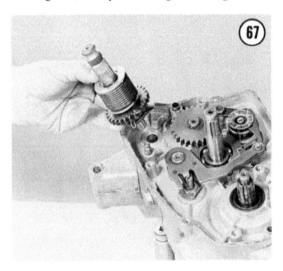

3. On some models, there is a shim between the crankcase and kickstarter shaft. Be careful not to lose it.

4. Remove the snap ring and thrust washer, then pull the kickstarter idler gear from its shaft (**Figure 68**).

Service

The kickstarter is a simple, rugged mechanism. The cause of any malfunction will be obvious upon examination. Check that all parts move freely, and that gear teeth are not excessively worn.

Installation

Kickstarter installation is generally the reverse of removal. Observe the following notes.

1. Be sure to install the shim mentioned under *Removal*, if your model was so equipped.

2. If your model has a clip (17, Figure 63), be sure that the end of it is inserted into the cavity in the crankcase. This cavity is at approximately 10 o'clock position.

3. Insert the end of the kick shaft halfway into its bore, connect the spring, then push the assembly inward until it is fully seated.

TACHOMETER DRIVE GEAR

Figure 69 is an exploded view of a typical tachometer drive mechanism. To remove the assembly, it is only necessary to take out the stopper retaining screw, then the housing, and finally the drive gear.

SHIFTER

Figure 70 illustrates a typical gearshift mechanism. As the rider presses the gearshift pedal, the shaft turns, and moves the gearshift arm.

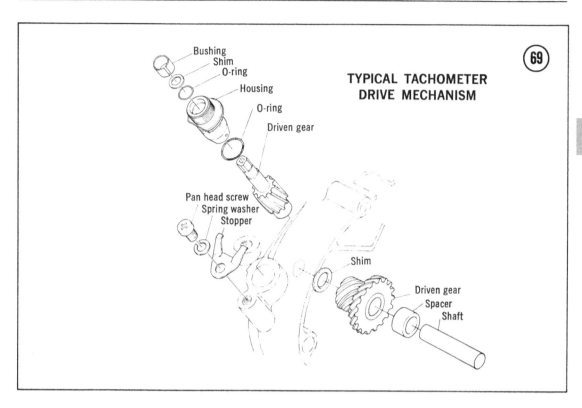

Bushing
Shim
O-ring
Housing
O-ring
Driven gear
Pan head screw
Spring washer
Stopper
Shim
Driven gear
Spacer
Shaft

**TYPICAL TACHOMETER
DRIVE MECHANISM**

69

3

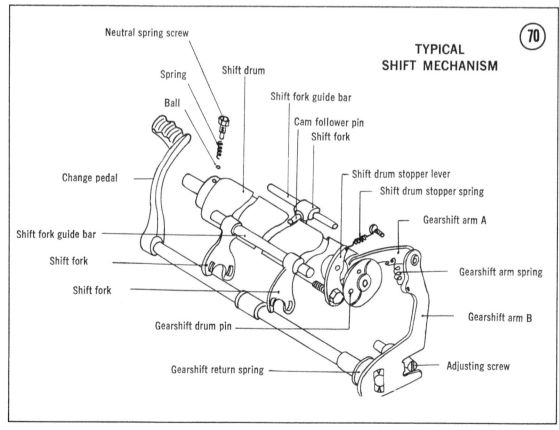

Neutral spring screw
Spring
Ball
Shift drum
Shift fork guide bar
Cam follower pin
Shift fork
Change pedal
Shift drum stopper lever
Shift drum stopper spring
Gearshift arm A
Shift fork guide bar
Shift fork
Shift fork
Gearshift arm spring
Gearshift drum pin
Gearshift arm B
Gearshift return spring
Adjusting screw

**TYPICAL
SHIFT MECHANISM**

70

The gearshift arm meshes with pins on the shift drum (part of the transmission assembly). Therefore, as the pedal is moved, the shift drum rotates. Grooves on the shift drum cause shift forks in the transmission to slide from side to side, thereby selecting the various gear ratios.

The stop lever also engages the pins on the change drum. They keep the drum in position after each step of rotation of the drum.

Table 9 lists the various types of shifters installed on models covered by this book. **Figures 71 through 76** are exploded views of those shifters. Refer to the applicable illustration during shifter service. Service procedures are similar for all models.

Table 9   SHIFTER TYPES

Model	Type	Figures	
AT series	1	71	72
CT series	1	71	72
DT125A	1	71	72
YZ100C	1	71	72
DT100A	2	73	74
MX100A	2	73	74
MX125A	2	73	74
DT175A	2	73	74
MX175A	2	73	74
GT series	3	75	76
YX80A	3	75	76

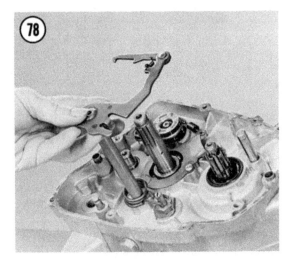

Removal

1. Remove the shifter shaft retaining clip (**Figure 77**) and washer from left side of engine.

2. Disengage gearshift arm from shift drum.

3. Pull out shifter shaft assembly (**Figure 78**).

4. Remove stop lever assembly (**Figure 79**).

5. Note how return spring is installed, then remove it (**Figure 80**).

Inspection

Check return spring tension. Replace the spring if it is weak or cracked. Inspect the stop lever spring for cracks or weakness. Be sure return spring pin is not loose. If it is, missed shifts will result. Be sure locknut is tight.

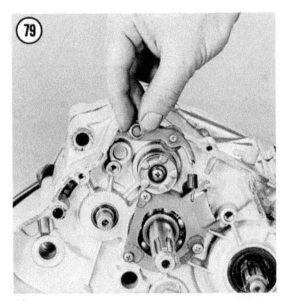

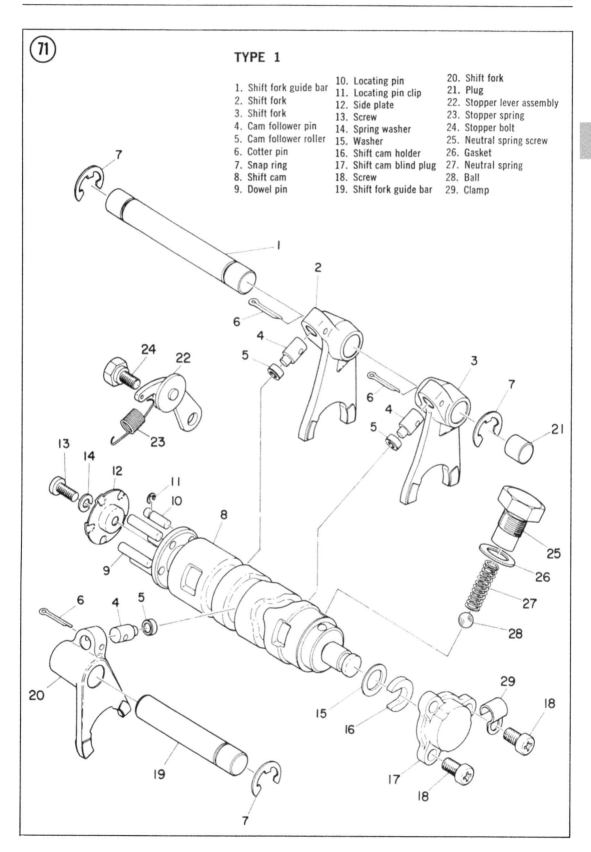

TYPE 1

1. Shift fork guide bar
2. Shift fork
3. Shift fork
4. Cam follower pin
5. Cam follower roller
6. Cotter pin
7. Snap ring
8. Shift cam
9. Dowel pin
10. Locating pin
11. Locating pin clip
12. Side plate
13. Screw
14. Spring washer
15. Washer
16. Shift cam holder
17. Shift cam blind plug
18. Screw
19. Shift fork guide bar
20. Shift fork
21. Plug
22. Stopper lever assembly
23. Stopper spring
24. Stopper bolt
25. Neutral spring screw
26. Gasket
27. Neutral spring
28. Ball
29. Clamp

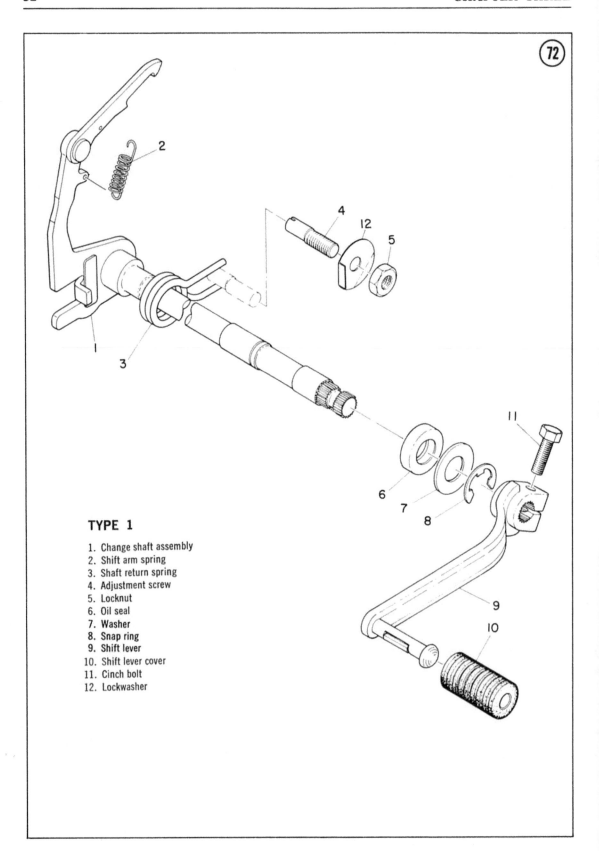

TYPE 1

1. Change shaft assembly
2. Shift arm spring
3. Shaft return spring
4. Adjustment screw
5. Locknut
6. Oil seal
7. Washer
8. Snap ring
9. Shift lever
10. Shift lever cover
11. Cinch bolt
12. Lockwasher

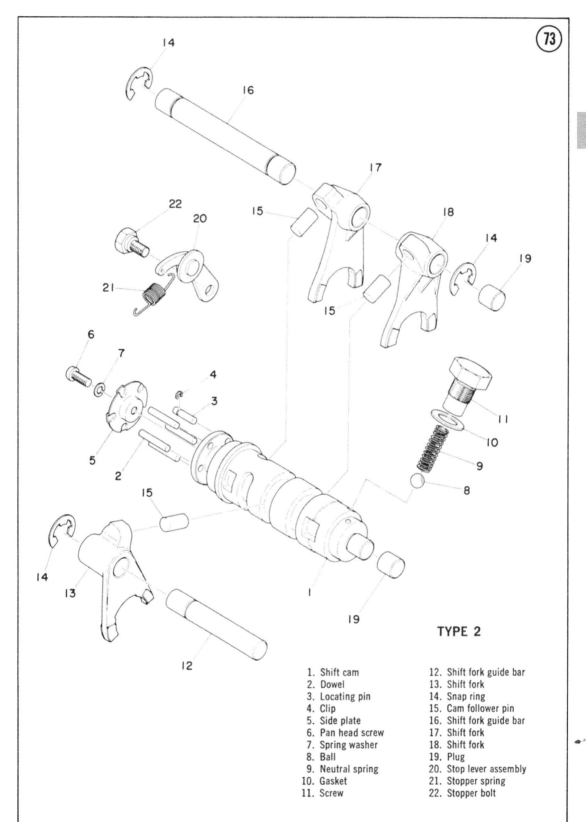

TYPE 2

1. Shift cam
2. Dowel
3. Locating pin
4. Clip
5. Side plate
6. Pan head screw
7. Spring washer
8. Ball
9. Neutral spring
10. Gasket
11. Screw
12. Shift fork guide bar
13. Shift fork
14. Snap ring
15. Cam follower pin
16. Shift fork guide bar
17. Shift fork
18. Shift fork
19. Plug
20. Stop lever assembly
21. Stopper spring
22. Stopper bolt

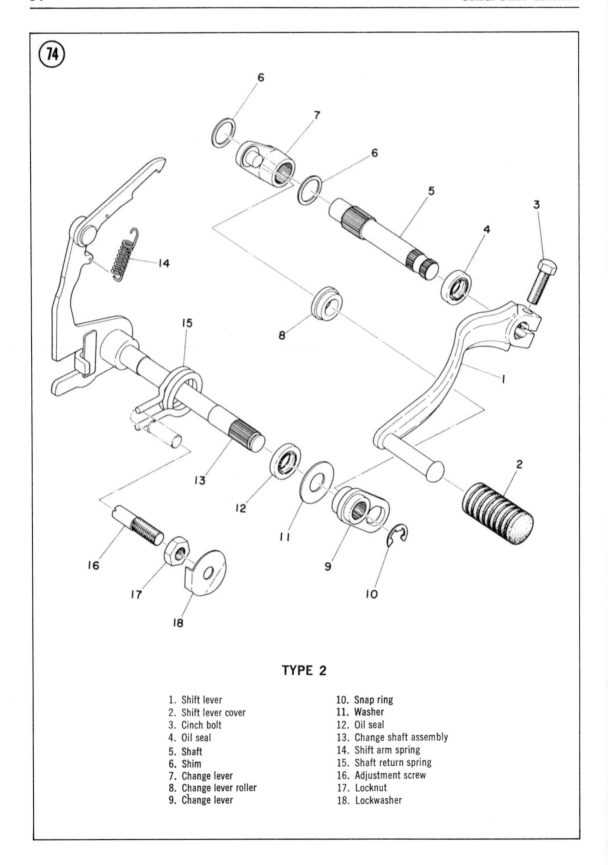

TYPE 2

1. Shift lever
2. Shift lever cover
3. Cinch bolt
4. Oil seal
5. Shaft
6. Shim
7. Change lever
8. Change lever roller
9. Change lever
10. Snap ring
11. Washer
12. Oil seal
13. Change shaft assembly
14. Shift arm spring
15. Shaft return spring
16. Adjustment screw
17. Locknut
18. Lockwasher

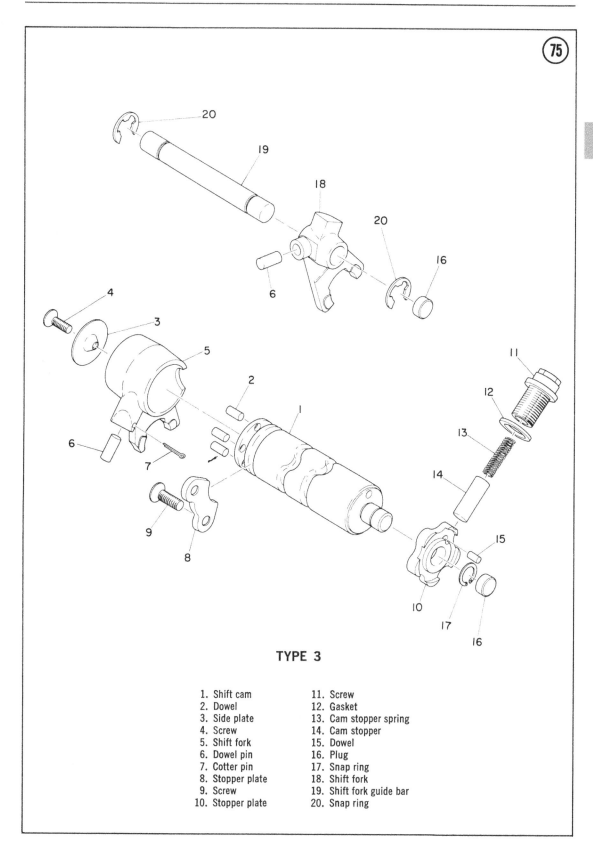

TYPE 3

1. Shift cam
2. Dowel
3. Side plate
4. Screw
5. Shift fork
6. Dowel pin
7. Cotter pin
8. Stopper plate
9. Screw
10. Stopper plate

11. Screw
12. Gasket
13. Cam stopper spring
14. Cam stopper
15. Dowel
16. Plug
17. Snap ring
18. Shift fork
19. Shift fork guide bar
20. Snap ring

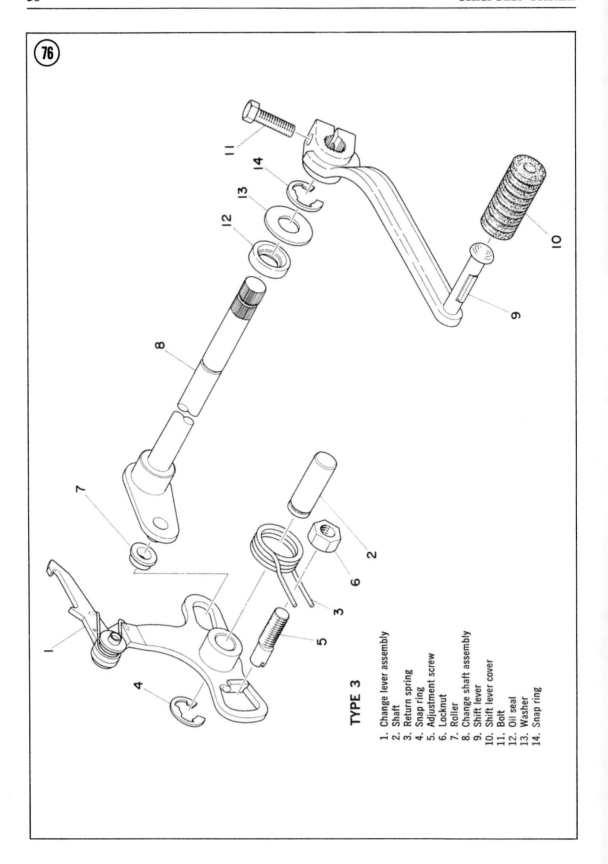

TYPE 3

1. Change lever assembly
2. Shaft
3. Return spring
4. Snap ring
5. Adjustment screw
6. Locknut
7. Roller
8. Change shaft assembly
9. Shift lever
10. Shift lever cover
11. Bolt
12. Oil seal
13. Washer
14. Snap ring

Installation

Reverse the removal procedure to install the shifter. Be sure that all springs are installed correctly.

Adjustment

The shifter must be adjusted under any of the following conditions:

    a. The transmission jumps out of gear.

    b. There is noticeable difference in shift lever travel between upshifts and downshifts.

    c. The shifter has been removed.

To adjust the shifter, refer to **Figure 81**, then proceed as follows.

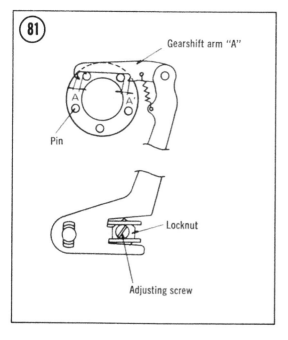

1. Loosen the locknut on the adjustment screw.

2. Turn the adjustment screw as required until distances A and A' are equal.

3. Hold the adjustment screw in position, then tighten the locknut. If there is a locking tab, bend it up.

To check this adjustment, gently push the shift lever up, then back to the at-rest position, then down and back. Push only until resistance is felt. The distance from at-rest to the upper point should equal the distance from at-rest to the lower position.

CRANKCASE

The crankcase is made in 2 halves of diecast aluminum alloy. They are assembled without a gasket; only gasket cement is used as a sealer. Dowel pins hold the crankcase halves in alignment when they are bolted together.

Separating Crankcase Halves

At this point, very few parts remain attached to the engine. These parts must be removed prior to engine case separation. Find your model in **Table 10**. After each model is a list of parts. An "X" in the table means that the part must be removed for that model.

Table 10   PARTS REMOVAL

Model	Stop	Stop Lever	Neutral Switch	Shift Cam Retainer
GT series	X	X		
AT, CT series, and MX's		X	X*	X
DT series				DT100 only
MX100, MX125, MX175, YZ125		X	neutral stop	

*Except MX.

1. Remove neutral switch (**Figure 82**).

2. Remove shift cam stop (**Figure 83**). There is a steel ball under this part. Remove it with a small magnet.

3. Remove shift cam retaining clip collar (**Figure 84**).

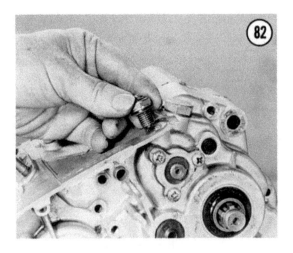

4. Remove cam retaining clip (**Figure 85**).

5. Remove all assembly screws. Loosen them in a crisscross pattern, a quarter turn at a time, until all are loose, to prevent warpage. **Figure 86** shows sample locations, which differ depending on your model.

> NOTE: *To prevent screw loss and to ensure proper location during assembly, draw a case outline on cardboard, then punch holes to correspond with screw locations. Insert removed screws in their appropriate locations.*

6. Install a crankcase separating tool, available at Yamaha dealers, on the right crankcase half. Be sure that both screws are in fully, then back one out as required until the tool is parallel with the crankcase.

7. Rotate the crankshaft to top dead center, then slowly turn the puller screw clockwise until both cases begin to separate (**Figure 87**).

8. Using a rubber or rawhide mallet, tap the crankcase half as required, so that it does not tilt. Also tap the transmission shaft and shift cam, if necessary, to ensure that they remain in the left crankcase.

CAUTION
Crankcase separation requires only hand pressure on the puller screw. If extreme pressure seems to be needed, or if both case halves will not remain parallel, stop immediately. Check for crankcase screws not removed, shift linkage still attached, or transmission shafts hung up in bearings. Relieve puller pressure immediately.

NOTE: *Never pry between case halves. Doing so may result in oil leaks, or could possibly result in other damage.*
Use only a rawhide or rubber mallet to tap case halves and transmission shafts.

9. As you lift off the separated case, immediately check for transmission shims that may stick to the inside of the transmission bearings (inside the case). If a shim is lost, stop assembly until it is found or replaced.

Inspection

1. Clean both case halves thoroughly with solvent to remove dirt, oil, and metal particles. Take particular care to prevent contamination of bearings.

2. Examine both crankcase mating surfaces carefully. Any damage to crank chamber sealing surfaces will result in lost crankcase compression and consequent poor running; other nicks or gouges in the transmission area may result in oil leaks.

3. Check that the transmission breather is not clogged. A clogged breather will result in pressure buildup and oil leakage.

4. Check crankshaft main bearings and transmission bearings for rust, wear, pitting, or excess radial clearance. If radial clearance of any bearing is more than 0.002 in. (0.5mm), replace

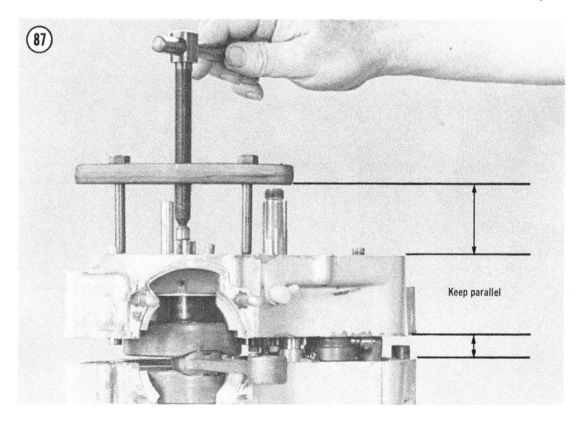

Keep parallel

the bearings. Before examining them, clean the bearings with solvent and dry them with compressed air, do not spin bearings with an air blast. Transmission bearings are particularly susceptible to damage from metal particles or other foreign material in the transmission oil. Crankshaft bearings may become damaged if the air filter is damaged or missing. **Figure 88** illustrates a crankshaft bearing which failed after only a few miles of operation without an air filter.

Assembly

1. Thoroughly clean both cases, then install transmission unit and crankshaft into the left case (see following sections on transmission and crankshaft for installation procedures).

2. Install all transmission and crankshaft shims.

3. Make sure all case locating dowel pins are installed, then place the right case down over the crankshaft and transmission shafts.

4. Apply sealing compound to both case mating surfaces. Follow the sealant manufacturer's application instructions. Place the transmission in NEUTRAL, then slide the right case half down into place, tapping it lightly, if necessary, with a rubber or rawhide mallet. If it does not seat easily, remove it, check for incorrect shim installation, or improperly installed parts.

5. Install all case screws. Tighten them in stages, in crisscross order, until all are firmly hand tight.

TRANSMISSION

Figures 89, 90, and 91 are exploded views of transmissions installed in Yamaha models covered by this manual.

> NOTE: *Models with a similar type have the same structural design but not necessarily the same dimensions or ratios.*

All transmissions are 4- or 5-speed units. Some gears are free to slide along splines on their respective shafts, and always turn with the shafts. There are dog clutches on these gears, which engage holes in other free-spinning gears. Splined gears are moved along their shafts by shift forks, which are controlled by a shift cam.

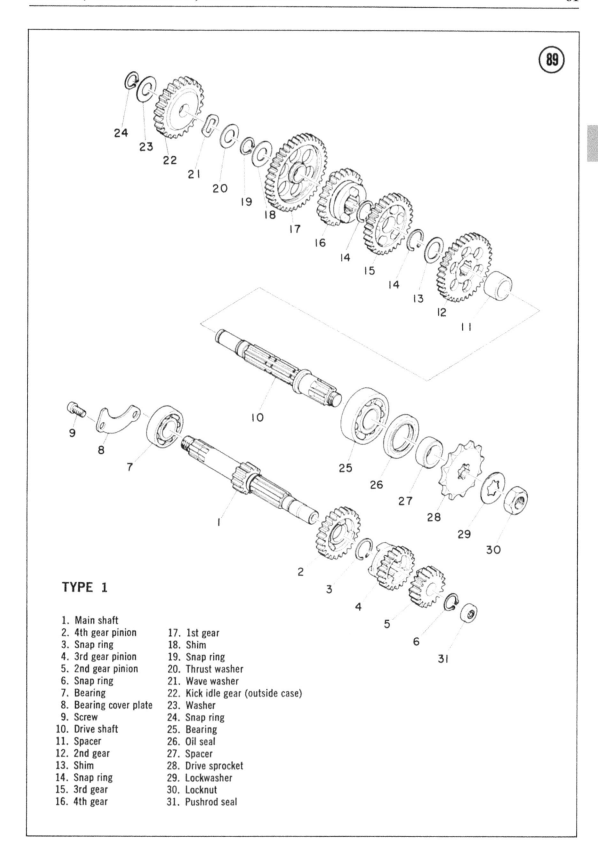

TYPE 1

1. Main shaft
2. 4th gear pinion
3. Snap ring
4. 3rd gear pinion
5. 2nd gear pinion
6. Snap ring
7. Bearing
8. Bearing cover plate
9. Screw
10. Drive shaft
11. Spacer
12. 2nd gear
13. Shim
14. Snap ring
15. 3rd gear
16. 4th gear
17. 1st gear
18. Shim
19. Snap ring
20. Thrust washer
21. Wave washer
22. Kick idle gear (outside case)
23. Washer
24. Snap ring
25. Bearing
26. Oil seal
27. Spacer
28. Drive sprocket
29. Lockwasher
30. Locknut
31. Pushrod seal

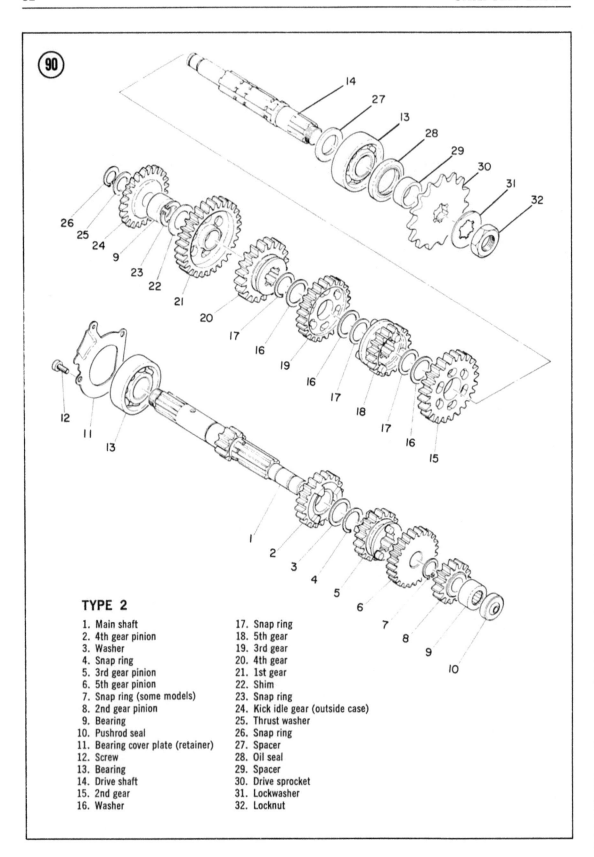

TYPE 2

1. Main shaft
2. 4th gear pinion
3. Washer
4. Snap ring
5. 3rd gear pinion
6. 5th gear pinion
7. Snap ring (some models)
8. 2nd gear pinion
9. Bearing
10. Pushrod seal
11. Bearing cover plate (retainer)
12. Screw
13. Bearing
14. Drive shaft
15. 2nd gear
16. Washer
17. Snap ring
18. 5th gear
19. 3rd gear
20. 4th gear
21. 1st gear
22. Shim
23. Snap ring
24. Kick idle gear (outside case)
25. Thrust washer
26. Snap ring
27. Spacer
28. Oil seal
29. Spacer
30. Drive sprocket
31. Lockwasher
32. Locknut

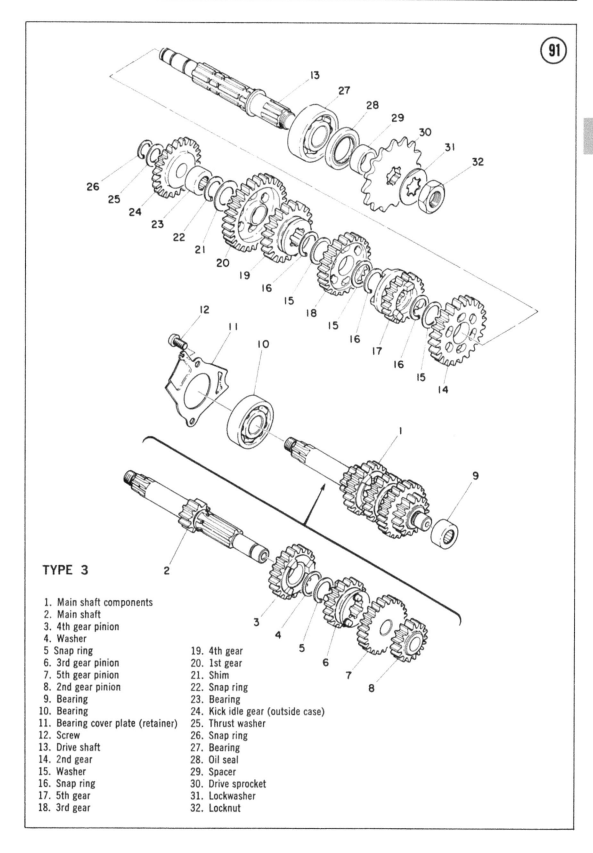

TYPE 3

1. Main shaft components
2. Main shaft
3. 4th gear pinion
4. Washer
5 Snap ring
6. 3rd gear pinion
7. 5th gear pinion
8. 2nd gear pinion
9. Bearing
10. Bearing
11. Bearing cover plate (retainer)
12. Screw
13. Drive shaft
14. 2nd gear
15. Washer
16. Snap ring
17. 5th gear
18. 3rd gear
19. 4th gear
20. 1st gear
21. Shim
22. Snap ring
23. Bearing
24. Kick idle gear (outside case)
25. Thrust washer
26. Snap ring
27. Bearing
28. Oil seal
29. Spacer
30. Drive sprocket
31. Lockwasher
32. Locknut

As one sliding splined gear is pulled out of engagement, because of shift drum rotation that moves the shift forks, another splined gear is pushed into engagement.

Neutral is established when the shift cam pulls all splined gears out of engagement simultaneously.

Figure 92 is a sectional view of a typical transmission. Arrows indicate movement of the various sliding gears within the transmission.

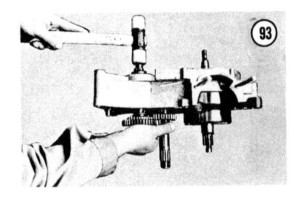

Removal

The following procedure applies to all models.
1. Support the left crankcase and hold the transmission assembly as shown in **Figure 93**. Using a rawhide or plastic mallet, tap both transmission shafts evenly from the case. Be sure to hold the entire transmission firmly to prevent parts from falling out prematurely. Take particular care not to let cam follower rollers (**Figure 94**) become lost.

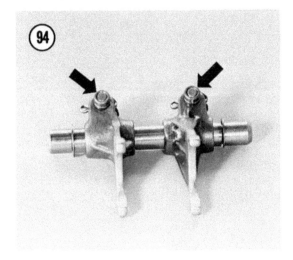

2. As individual parts are disassembled, lay them out in order of their removal, and make a rough sketch of parts layout, if necessary. This procedure will greatly assist in transmission reassembly, especially if considerable time elapses before installation.

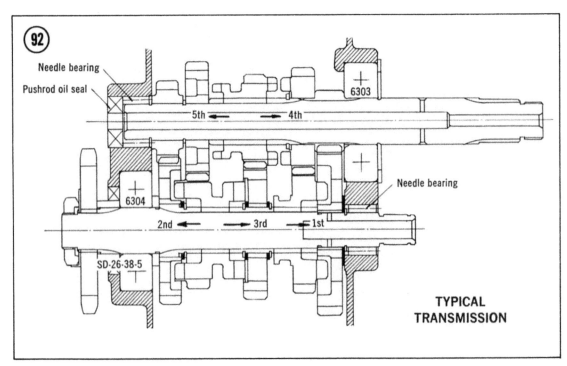

Needle bearing
Pushrod oil seal
6303
5th — 4th
Needle bearing
6304
2nd — 3rd — 1st
SD-26-38-5

TYPICAL TRANSMISSION

3. If it is necessary to remove second gear from the main shaft on transmission types 2 and 3, support the gear evenly around its circumference, then press the main shaft out. Upon reassembly, press the gear to within 0.002 in. (0.05mm) of fifth gear. Heating the gear to approximately 200°F (95°C) and chilling the main shaft before installation will make reassembly easier.

Inspection

1. Slide each splined gear along its shaft. Gears must operate smoothly. Minor roughness may be smoothed with an oilstone. Replace the gear and/or the shaft in the event of severe damage.

2. Check each gear for chipped or cracked teeth, or cracked wall sections. Replace any damaged gear.

3. Check dog clutches for rounded teeth, and also check that they engage properly. Replace gears with severely rounded clutch teeth.

4. Measure clearance between each shift fork and its associated gear (**Figure 95**). Any clearance greater than 0.024 in. (0.6mm) should be considered excessive. Replace the gear and/or shift fork in that event.

5. Be sure that shift forks are not bent or burned. Replace shift forks if their condition is doubtful.

6. Replace any shift fork guide bar that is bent. Roll it across a flat surface to check for straightness.

7. Mount each transmission shaft in V-blocks or other suitable centering device, then check them for straightness. Replace any shaft if it is bent more than 0.0008 in. (0.02mm).

8. Thoroughly clean transmission bearings, then oil them lightly. Rotate their inner races, and check them for rough operation. If any roughness is evident, and it cannot be eliminated by thorough cleaning, replace the bearing.

Installation

1. Assemble the transmission, shift forks, and shift cam into a single unit, as it was when it was removed.

2. Install the assembled transmission into the left crankcase. It may be necessary to tap it into place with a plastic or other soft-faced mallet.

End Play Adjustment

Whenever the transmission is disassembled, or it jumps out of gear for no apparent reason, transmission shaft end play should be checked, and adjusted if necessary.

End play of both shafts must be 0.002-0.008 in. (0.05-0.20mm).

1. Main shaft end play is taken up automatically when the clutch retaining nut is tightened. If there was a factory-installed shim on the right side of the main shaft, be sure that it is in place.

2. Refer to **Figure 96**. Measure across the entire width of the assembled countershaft, including all snap rings and existing shims. Record this measurement, calling it "dimension A".

3. Measure depth of each crankcase half, from its mating surface to surface of the inner bearing race that supports the shaft (**Figure 97**).

4. From each measured depth, subtract the thickness of the parallels used to support the depth gauge. Call these measurements "dimensions B and C".

5. Add the depth of each crankcase half (dimensions B and C) to obtain the total distance between bearings when the crankcase is assembled.

6. Subtract assembled transmission shaft width (dimension A) from combined crankcase depth measurement. The difference between these measurements is shaft end play.

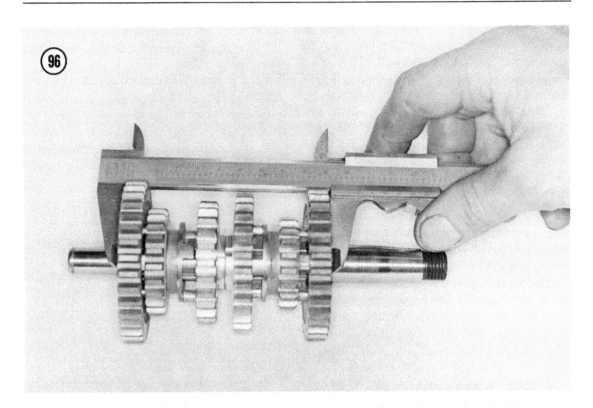

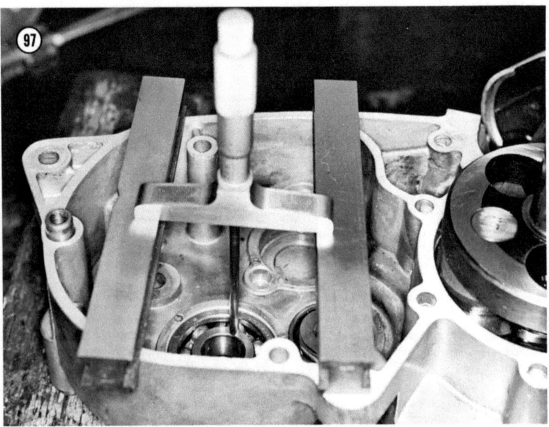

Example:

Width of shaft assembly 5.978 (dimension A)

Depth to left bearing   3.748
Less thickness of parallels 0.750
                           ───────
                           2.998 (dimension B)

Depth to right bearing   3.750
Less thickness of parallels 0.750
                           ───────
                           3.000 (dimension C)

Add dimensions B and C   2.998
                          3.000
                          ───────
                          5.998 (crankcase width)

Subtract dimension A from
    total crankcase width:
                          5.998
                          5.978
                          ───────
                          0.020 (total end play)

Desired end play is 0.002-0.008 in. There-fore, to determine total additional shim thick-ness for that shaft, subtract desired end play (0.004 in., for example) from total end play.

                  0.020 (total end play)
                  0.004 (desired end play)
                  ───────
                  0.016 (total shims required)

Add shims totaling 0.016 in. to the shaft in question. Divide the shims equally on both ends of the shaft. Shims are available at Yamaha dealers.

Troubleshooting

1. *Jumping out of gear.* When this situation occurs, the normal correction procedure is to replace both gears, plus the associated shift fork. This problem almost always results in damage to each component. Failure to replace any of them could cause the problem to reoccur rapidly.

2. *Pressed-on second gear spinning.* On models with pressed-on second gear, it is not uncommon for this gear to spin, get hot, and gall. As the gear cools, it fuses to its shaft. This situation is not necessarily cause for gear and main shaft replacement, unless second gear continually slips.

CRANKSHAFT

The crankshaft operates under conditions of high stress. Dimensional tolerances are critical.

It is necessary to locate and correct defects in the crankshaft to prevent more serious trouble later. **Figure 98** illustrates parts of a typical crankshaft assembly.

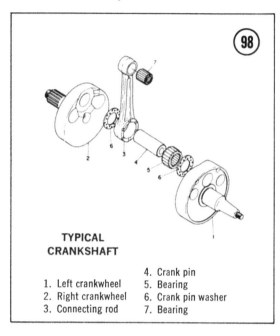

**TYPICAL
CRANKSHAFT**

1. Left crankwheel
2. Right crankwheel
3. Connecting rod
4. Crank pin
5. Bearing
6. Crank pin washer
7. Bearing

Removal

Start the crankshaft from the left crankcase, using the crankcase separating tool. Be sure that both bolts on the tool are fully tightened, and that the tool remains parallel to the crank-case, so that no side force is exerted on the crankshaft. Once the crankshaft is free from the left main bearing, lift it from the crankcase (**Figure 99**).

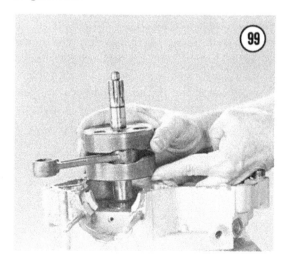

Inspection

There are several measurement locations on the crankshaft assembly. Measurements to be made are big end radial clearance, big end side clearance, and small end radial clearance.

Since it is difficult to measure big end radial clearance directly, measure the distance that the upper end of the connecting rod moves sideways when the lower end is held to one side (**Figure 100**). Side-to-side movement of the upper end should not exceed 0.079 in. (0.20mm).

NOTE: *Do not mistake lower end side play for upper end motion.*

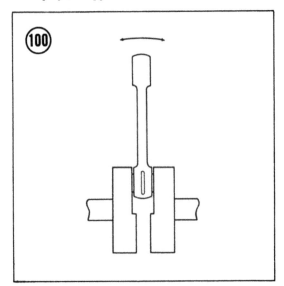

crankshaft through a complete revolution and measure runout at the main bearing journals, as shown in **Figure 102**. If the dial indicator reading is greater than the repair limit, disassemble the crankshaft and replace the crankpin. If runout exceeds the standard limit, but does not exceed the repair limit, it may be corrected. Standard runout limit for all models is 0.0012 in. (0.03mm). The repair limit is 0.004 in. (0.10mm) for all models.

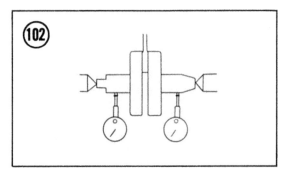

Measure lower end side play as shown in **Figure 101**. Side clearance on a new or rebuilt crankshaft should be 0.016-0.020 in. (0.40-0.50mm). Rebuild or exchange the crankshaft if side clearance is 0.023 in. (0.60mm) or greater.

To measure small end radial clearance, clean and dry the piston pin, upper end bearing, and connecting rod. Assemble them without lubrication. Then check for any perceptible play in the upper end. If any exists, replace the piston pin and bearing. In extreme cases it may be necessary to replace the connecting rod also.

Crankshaft Runout

Mount the crankshaft in a lathe, V-blocks, or other suitable centering device. Rotate the

Crankshaft Overhaul

Crankshaft overhaul requires a press of 10-12 tons (9,000-11,000 kg) capacity, holding jigs, and a crankshaft alignment jig. Do not attempt to overhaul the crankshaft unless this equipment is available.

1. Place the crankshaft assembly in a suitable jig, then press out the crankpin from the drive side first (**Figure 103**).

2. Remove the spacers, connecting rod, and lower end bearing (**Figure 104**).

3

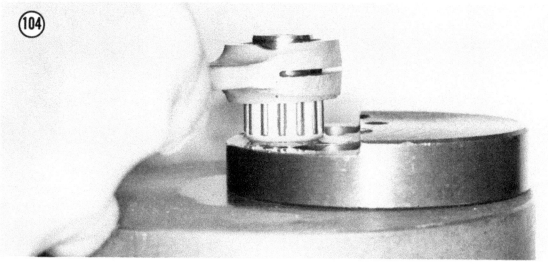

3. Press the crankpin out from the magneto side (**Figure 105**).

4. Carefully remove all residue from the crank wheels.

5. Using a suitable alignment fixture, press the replacement crankpin into the magneto side crank wheel (**Figure 106**) until the end of the crankpin is flush with the outside of the crank wheel.

6. Install a side washer, then the bearing.

7. Install the connecting rod then the remaining side washer. There is no front or back to the connecting rod; it fits either way.

8. Using a small square for initial alignment (**Figure 107**), start pressing the drive side crank wheel onto the crankpin.

9. Insert a 0.016 in. feeler gauge between the upper spacer and drive side crank wheel. Con-

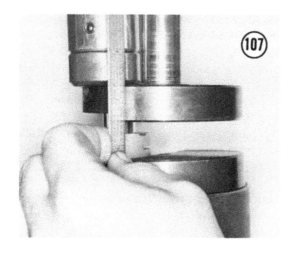

tinue pressing the drive side crank wheel onto the crankpin until the feeler gauge fits tightly.

10. Release all pressure from the press. The feeler gauge will then slip out easily.

11. Align the crankshaft assembly.

If after a crankshaft seizure, either crankshaft half is damaged, replace the entire crankshaft assembly. Otherwise, disassemble the crankshaft and replace the connecting rod, needle bearing, side washers, and crankpin.

Defective crankshaft seals are the most common cause of catastrophic crankshaft failures. Always replace crankcase oil seals when the crankshaft is removed for service.

Crankshaft Alignment

After any crankshaft service, it is necessary to align the assembly so that both crank wheels and the shafts extending from them all rotate on a common center. Mount the assembled crankshaft in a suitable alignment fixture, as described under *Crankshaft Runout*, then slowly rotate the crankshaft through one or more complete turns, and observe both dial indicators. One of several indications will be observed.

1. Neither dial indicator needle begins its swing at the same time, and the needles will move in opposite directions during part of the crankshaft rotation cycle. Each needle will probably indicate a different amount of total travel. This condition is caused by eccentricity (both crank wheels not being on the same center, as shown in **Figure 108**). To correct this situation, slowly rotate the crankshaft assembly until the drive side dial gauge indicates its maximum. Mark the rim of the drive side crank wheel at the

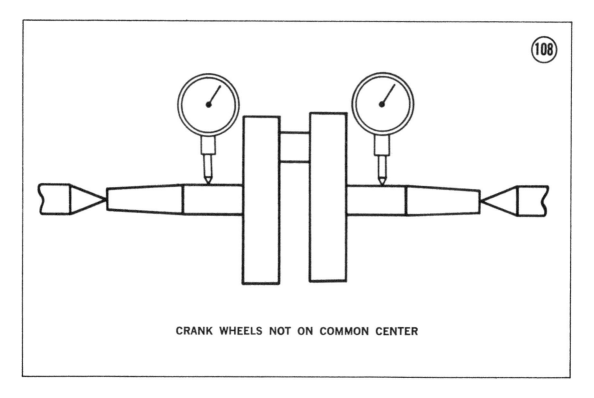

CRANK WHEELS NOT ON COMMON CENTER

point in line with the plungers on both dial gauges. Remove the crankshaft assembly from the jig, then while holding the magneto side crank wheel in one hand, strike the chalk mark a sharp blow with a brass or lead mallet (**Figure 109**). Recheck alignment after each blow, and continue this procedure until both dial gauges begin and end their swings at the same time.

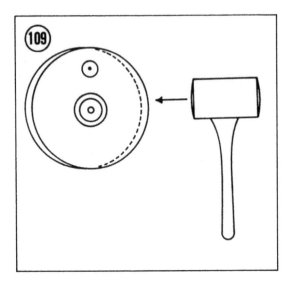

2. After the foregoing adjustment is completed, the crank wheels may still be pinched, as shown in **Figure 110**, or spread (**Figure 111**). Both dial indicators will indicate maximum travel when the crankpin is toward the dial gauges if the crank wheels are pinched. Correct this condition by removing the crankshaft assembly, then drive a wedge or chisel between the crank wheels at a point opposite maximum dial gauge indication. Recheck alignment after each adjustment. Continue this procedure until the dial gauges indicate no more than 0.0012 in. (0.03mm) run-out on each side.

If the dial gauges indicate their maximum when the crankpin is on the side of the alignment test jig away from the dial gauges, the crank wheels are spread. Correct this condition by tapping the outside of one of the wheels toward the other with a brass or lead mallet. Recheck alignment after each blow. Continue adjustment until runout is within the tolerance specified in the foregoing paragraph.

NOTE: *It may be necessary to repeat the correction for eccentricity during the correction procedure for pinch or spread.*

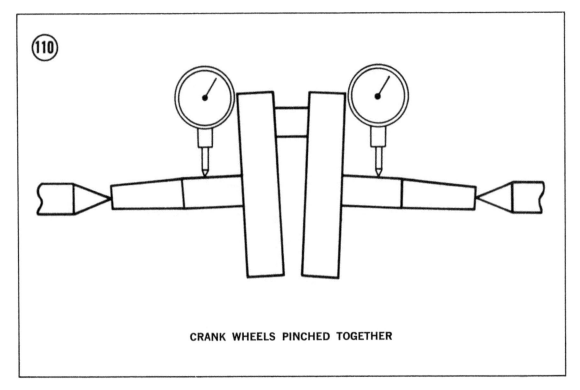

CRANK WHEELS PINCHED TOGETHER

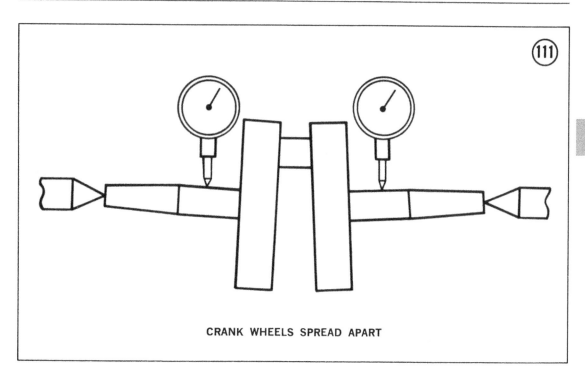

CRANK WHEELS SPREAD APART

CHAPTER FOUR

CARBURETORS

This chapter discusses carburetor operating principles, service, adjustment, and troubleshooting.

CARBURETOR OPERATION

For proper operation, a gasoline engine must be supplied with fuel and air, mixed in proper proportions by weight. A mixture in which there is an excess of fuel is said to be rich. A lean mixture is one which contains insufficient fuel. It is the function of the carburetor to supply the proper mixture to the engine under all operating conditions.

Essential functional parts of Mikuni carburetors are a float and float valve mechanism for maintaining a constant fuel level in the float bowl, a pilot system for supplying fuel at low speeds, a main fuel system which supplies the engine at medium and high speeds, and a starter system which supplies the very rich mixture needed to start a cold engine. Operation of each system is discussed in the following paragraphs.

Float Mechanism

Figure 1 illustrates a typical float mechanism. Proper operation of the carburetor is dependent on maintaining a constant fuel level in the car-

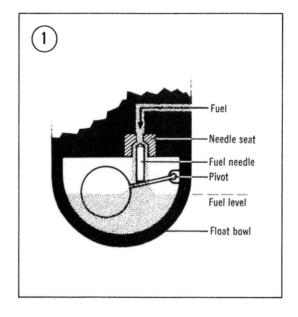

- Fuel
- Needle seat
- Fuel needle
- Pivot
- Fuel level
- Float bowl

buretor bowl. As fuel is drawn from the float bowl, float level drops. When the float drops, the float valve moves away from its seat and allows fuel to flow past the valve and seat into the float bowl. As this occurs, the float rises, pressing the float needle against its seat, thereby shutting off fuel flow. It can be seen from this discussion that a small piece of dirt can be trapped between the float needle and its seat, preventing the valve from closing and allowing fuel to rise beyond the normal level, resulting in flooding. **Figure 2** illustrates this condition.

Pilot System

Under idle or low speed conditions, at less than ⅛ throttle, the engine does not require much fuel or air, and the throttle valve is almost closed. A separate pilot system is required for operation under such conditions. **Figure 3** illustrates pilot system operation. Air is drawn through the pilot air inlet and controlled by the pilot air screw. This air is then mixed with fuel drawn through the pilot jet. The air/fuel mixture then travels from the pilot outlet into the main air passage, where it is further mixed with air prior to being drawn into the engine. The pilot air screw controls idle mixture.

If proper idle and low speed mixture cannot be obtained within normal adjustment range of the idle mixture screw, refer to **Table 1** for possible causes.

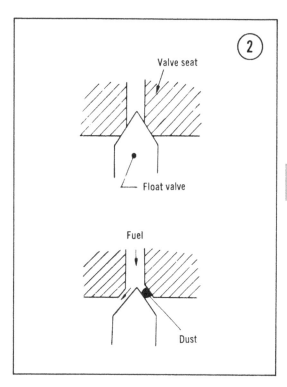

CARBURETOR OPERATION
(THROTTLE OPENING 0 TO ⅛)

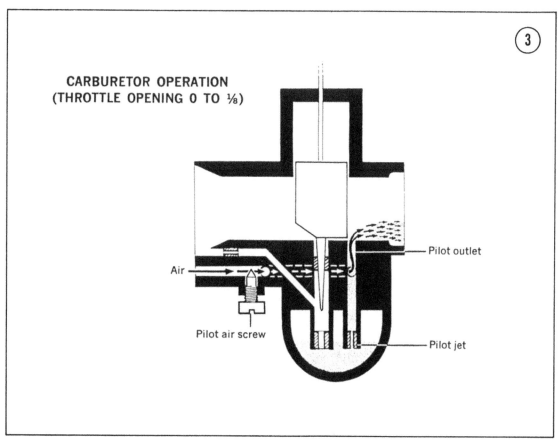

Table 1   IDLE MIXTURE TROUBLESHOOTING

Too Rich
Clogged pilot air intake
Clogged air passage
Clogged air bleed opening
Pilot jet loose
Starter lever not returned
Starter plunger not closed
Starter cable misadjusted

Too Lean
Obstructed pilot jet
Obstructed jet outlet
Worn throttle valve
Carburetor mounting loose

Main Fuel System

As the throttle is opened still more, up to about ¼ open, the pilot circuit begins to supply less of the mixture to the engine, as the main fuel system, illustrated in **Figure 4**, begins to function. The main jet, needle jet, jet needle, and air jet make up the main fuel circuit. As the throttle valve opens more than about ⅛ of its travel, air is drawn through the main port, and passes under the throttle valve in the main bore. Air stream velocity results in reduced pressure around the jet needle. Fuel then passes through the main jet, past the needle jet and jet needle, and into the main air stream where it is atomized and then drawn into the cylinder. As the throttle valve opens, more air flows through the carburetor, and the jet needle, which is attached to the throttle slide, rises to permit more fuel to flow.

A portion of the air bled past the air jet passes through the needle jet bleed air inlet into the needle jet, where the air is mixed with the main air stream and atomized.

Airflow at small throttle openings is controlled primarily by the cutaway on the throttle slide.

As the throttle is opened wider, up to about ¾ open, the circuit draws air from 2 sources,

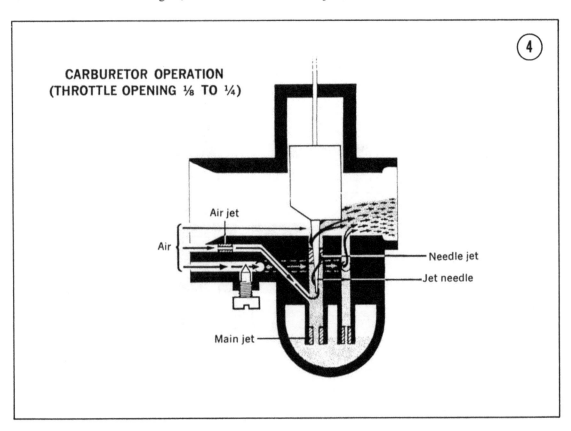

CARBURETOR OPERATION
(THROTTLE OPENING ⅛ TO ¼)

Air jet

Air

Needle jet

Jet needle

Main jet

as shown in **Figure 5**. The first source is air passing through the venturi; the second source is through the air jet. Air passing through the venturi draws fuel through the needle jet. The jet needle is tapered, and therefore allows more fuel to pass. Air passing through the air jet passes to the needle jet to aid atomization of the fuel there.

Figure 6 illustrates the circuit at high speeds. The jet needle is withdrawn almost completely from the needle jet. Fuel flow is then controlled by the main jet. Air passing through the air jet continues to aid atomization of the fuel as described in the foregoing paragraphs.

Any dirt which collects in the main jet or in the needle jet obstructs fuel flow and causes a lean mixture. Any clogged air passage, such as the air bleed opening or air jet, may result in an overrich mixture. Other causes of a rich mixture are a worn needle jet, loose needle jet, or loose main jet. If the jet needle is worn, it should be replaced; however it may be possible to effect a temporary repair by placing the needle jet clip in a higher groove.

Starter System

A cold engine requires a fuel mixture much richer than that normally required. The starter system provides this mixture. A typical system is shown in **Figure 7**.

When the rider operates the starter lever, starter plunger (13) is pulled upward. As the engine is cranked, suction from the engine draws fuel through starter jet (10). This fuel is then mixed with air from bleed air port (11) in float chamber (12). This mixture is further mixed with primary air coming through air passage (14), and is then delivered to the engine through port (15) behind the throttle valve. Note that the mixture from the starter system is mixed with that from the pilot system.

CARBURETOR OVERHAUL

There is no set rule regarding frequency of carburetor overhaul. A carburetor used on a machine used for street riding may go 5,000 miles without attention. If the machine is used in dirt, the carburetor might need an overhaul

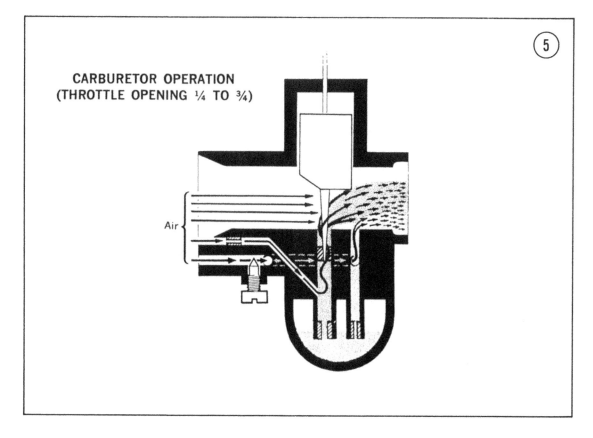

CARBURETOR OPERATION
(THROTTLE OPENING ¼ TO ¾)

Air

5

CHAPTER FOUR

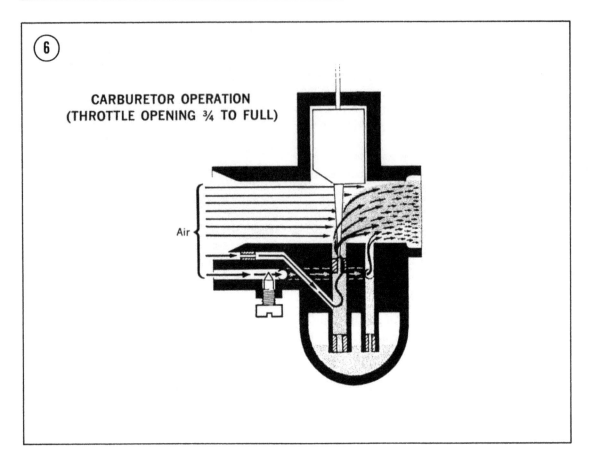

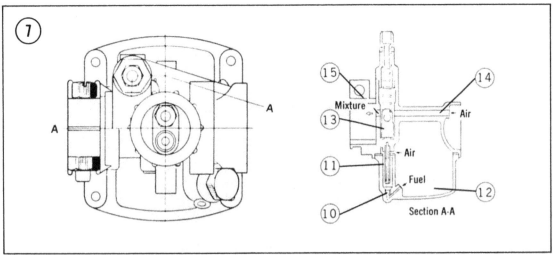

in less than 1,000 miles. Poor engine performance, hesitation, and little or no response to mixture adjustment are all symptoms of possible carburetor malfunctions. In general, it is good practice to overhaul the carburetor each time you perform a routine engine decarbonization.

Remove the carburetor from the engine and disassemble it. Shake the float to check for gasoline inside. If fuel leaks into the float, the float chamber fuel level will rise, resulting in an overrich mixture. Replace the float if it is deformed or leaking.

Replace the float valve if its seating end is scratched or worn. Press the float valve gently with your finger and make sure that the valve seats properly. If the float valve does not seat properly, fuel will overflow, causing an over-rich mixture and flooding the float chamber whenever the fuel petcock is open.

Clean all parts in carburetor cleaning solvent. Dry the parts with compressed air. Clean jets and other delicate parts with compressed air after the float bowl has been removed. Use new gaskets upon reassembly.

Never blow compressed air into any assembled carburetor; doing so may result in damage to the float needle valve.

Always check float level after carburetor overhaul, and readjust if necessary. Refer to *Float Level*.

Mikuni carburetors are supplied as standard equipment on Yamaha motorcycles. They can be classified by float type; some models have independent floats, and others have single-unit, or twin floats.

Independent Float Carburetors

Figure 8 is an exploded view of this type carburetor. Refer to that illustration during disassembly and reassembly.

1. Remove mixing chamber cap **(Figure 9)**. There is a spring under the cap; do not allow any parts to fly away.

2. Remove throttle slide assembly **(Figure 10)**.
3. Remove float bowl **(Figure 11)**.
4. Remove floats **(Figure 12)**.
5. Remove main jet **(Figure 13)**.

6. Remove pivot pin and float lever **(Figure 14)**. Note carefully how float lever is installed; it is possible to reassemble this component upside down.

7. Remove float needle retainer, then float needle **(Figure 15)**. Upon reassembly, install float needle retainer as shown in **Figure 16**.

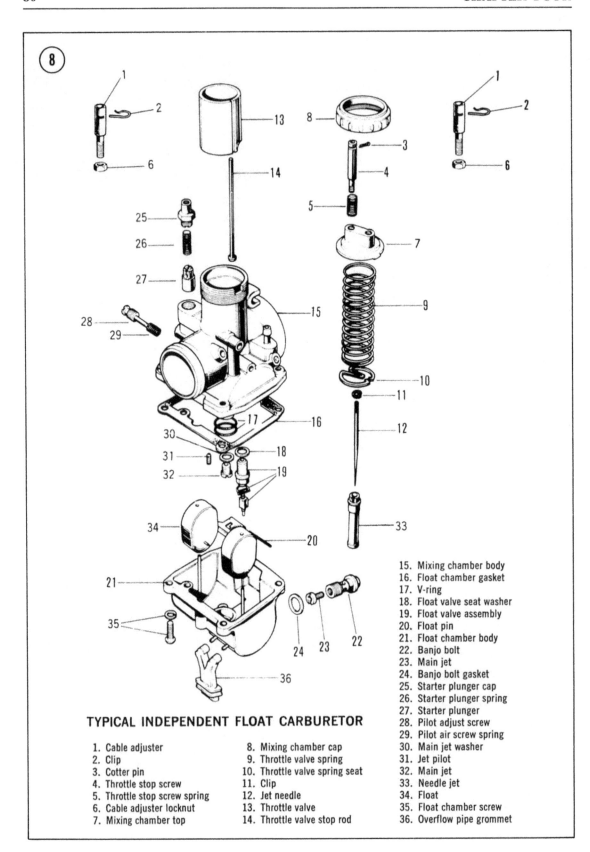

TYPICAL INDEPENDENT FLOAT CARBURETOR

1. Cable adjuster
2. Clip
3. Cotter pin
4. Throttle stop screw
5. Throttle stop screw spring
6. Cable adjuster locknut
7. Mixing chamber top
8. Mixing chamber cap
9. Throttle valve spring
10. Throttle valve spring seat
11. Clip
12. Jet needle
13. Throttle valve
14. Throttle valve stop rod
15. Mixing chamber body
16. Float chamber gasket
17. V-ring
18. Float valve seat washer
19. Float valve assembly
20. Float pin
21. Float chamber body
22. Banjo bolt
23. Main jet
24. Banjo bolt gasket
25. Starter plunger cap
26. Starter plunger spring
27. Starter plunger
28. Pilot adjust screw
29. Pilot air screw spring
30. Main jet washer
31. Jet pilot
32. Main jet
33. Needle jet
34. Float
35. Float chamber screw
36. Overflow pipe grommet

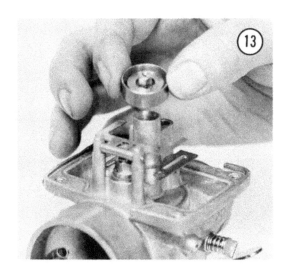

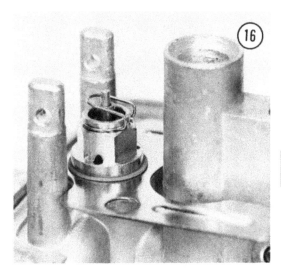

8. Remove float valve seat. If there is a plate underneath it, remove plate also (**Figure 17**). Note how washer is installed.

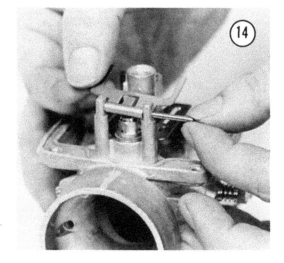

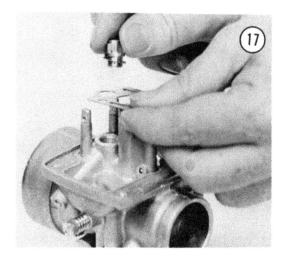

9. Remove pilot jet (**Figure 18**).

10. Invert carburetor, then push out needle jet (**Figure 19**). Do not use any metal tool for this operation.

11. Remove idle speed and mixture screws.

Single-Unit Float Carburetors

Figure 20 is an exploded view of a typical carburetor of this type. Refer to that illustration during disassembly and reassembly.

1. Remove mixing chamber cap (**Figure 21**).

2. Remove throttle valve assembly (**Figure 22**).

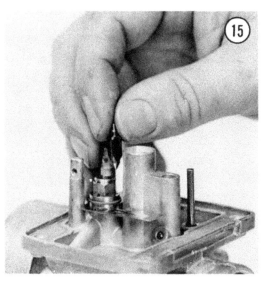

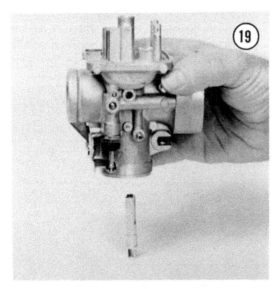

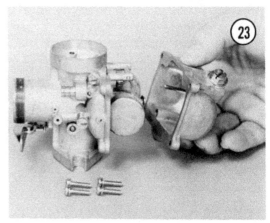

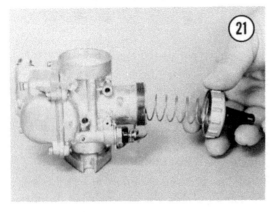

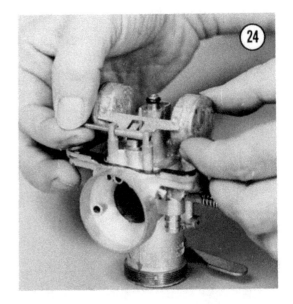

3. Remove float bowl (**Figure 23**).

4. Remove pivot pin and float (**Figure 24**). Take care not to bend float assembly.

5. Remove float needle (**Figure 25**).

6. Remove main jet and its washer (**Figure 26**).

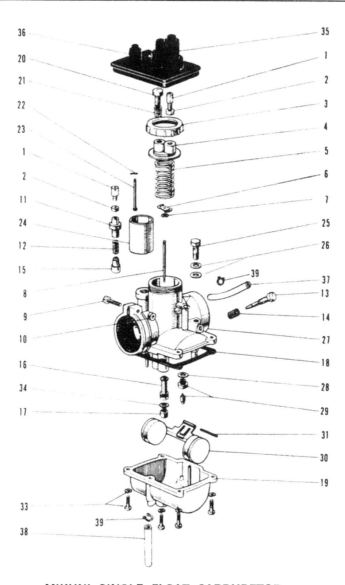

MIKUNI SINGLE FLOAT CARBURETOR

1. Cable adjuster
2. Cable adjuster lock nut
3. Mixing chamber cap
4. Mixing chamber top
5. Throttle valve spring
6. Throttle valve spring seat
7. Needle clip
8. Jet needle
9. Carburetor mounting clamp screw
10. Nut
11. Starter plunger cap
12. Starter plunger spring
13. Pilot air adjusting screw
14. Pilot air adjusting screw spring
15. Starter plunger
16. Needle jet
17. Main jet
18. Float chamber gasket
19. Float chamber body
20. Throttle adjuster
21. Throttle adjuster spring
22. Cotter pin
23. Throttle valve stop rod
24. Throttle valve
25. Banjo bolt
26. Gasket
27. Mixing chamber body
28. Float valve seat washer
29. Float valve complete
30. Float
31. Float pin
33. Float chamber fitting screw
34. Main jet washer
35. Carburetor cap grommet
36. Carburetor cap
37. Fuel overflow pipe
38. Air vent pipe
39. Circlip

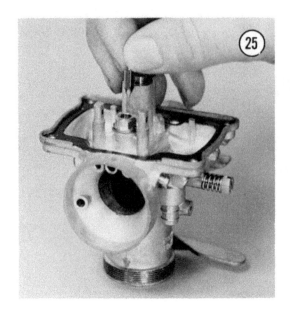

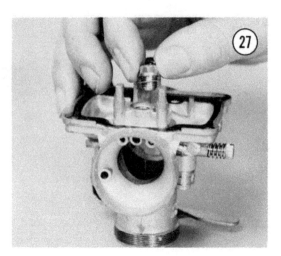

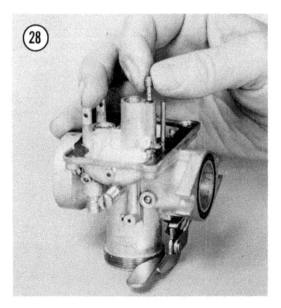

7. Remove float valve seat and its washer (**Figure 27**).

8. Remove pilot jet (**Figure 28**).

9. Push out needle jet, using a plastic or fiber tool (**Figure 29**).

10. Remove idle speed and idle mixture screws. Take care not to lose their springs.

CARBURETOR ADJUSTMENT

The carburetor was designed to provide the proper mixture under all operating conditions. Little or no benefit will result from experiment-ing. However, unusual operating conditions such as sustained operation at high altitudes, or unusually high or low temperatures, may make modifications to standard specifications desir-able. The adjustments described in the following paragraphs should only be undertaken if the rider has definite reason to believe they are required. Make the tests and adjustments in the order specified. Float level should be checked each time the carburetor is disassembled, and adjusted if necessary.

Float Level

Mikuni carburetors with independent floats leave the factory with float levels properly ad-

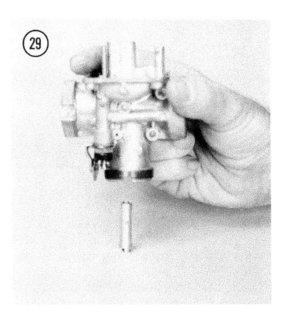

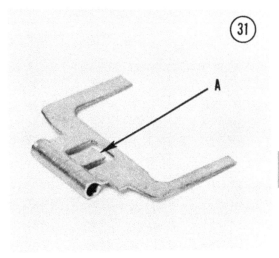

A. Bend tang to adjust float level

justed. Rough riding, a worn needle valve, or a bent float arm can cause the float level to change. To adjust float level on these carburetors, refer to **Figure 30**, then proceed as follows.

1. Remove the float bowl and floats, then invert the carburetor body. Allow the float lever to rest on the needle by its own weight.

2. Measure the distance from the float arm to the carburetor body surface.

3. Bend the tang on the float arm (**Figure 31**) as required for adjustment.

4. Float levels are specified in **Table 2**.

To adjust float level on carburetors with single-unit floats, refer to **Figure 32**, then proceed as follows.

1. Remove the float chamber and invert the mixer body. Allow the float arm to rest on the needle valve by its own weight, without compressing the float needle spring.

2. Measure distance (A) from the top of the floats to the float bowl gasket surface. Note that distance (A) must be equal for each float.

3. Bend the tang on the float arm (**Figure 33**) as required for adjustment.

4. Float levels are specified in Table 2.

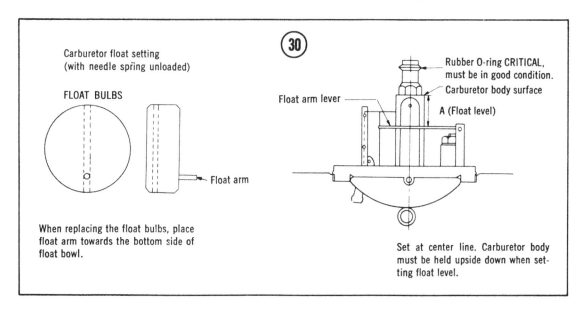

Table 2   FLOAT LEVEL

Model	Inches	(Millimeters)
GT series	0.83	(21.0)
YZ80A	0.91	(23.0)
DT100A	0.79*	(20.0)*
MX100A	0.62	(15.8)
AT1 series (and MX)	1.00	(25.5)
AT2, AT3	0.83	(21.0)
AT2-MX	0.98	(25.0)
ATMX	0.98	(25.0)
DT125A	0.79*	(20.0)*
MX125A	0.62*	(15.8)*
YZ100C	0.59*	(15.0)*
YZ125A	0.62*	(15.8)
CT1 series	1.00	(25.5)
CT2, CT3	0.83	(21.0)
DT125A	0.79*	(20.0)*
MX175A	0.62	(15.8)*

*Measured from base gasket surface to float arm lever.

A. Bend tang to adjust float level

are the main jet, needle jet, jet needle and clip, and throttle valve.

Make a road test at full throttle for final determination of main jet size. To make such a test, operate the motorcycle at full throttle for at least 2 minutes, then shut the engine off, release the clutch, and bring the machine to a stop.

If at full throttle, the engine runs "heavily," the main jet is too large. If the engine runs better by closing the throttle slightly, the main jet is too small. The engine will run at full throttle evenly and regularly if the main jet is of correct size.

After each such test, remove and examine the spark plug. The insulator should have a light tan color. If the insulator has black sooty deposits, the mixture is too rich. If there are signs of intense heat, such as a blistered white appearance, the mixture is too lean.

As a general rule, main jet size should be reduced approximately 5 percent for each 3,000 feet (1,000 meters) above sea level.

Table 3 lists symptoms caused by rich and lean mixtures.

Adjust the pilot air screw as follows.

1. Turn pilot air screw in until it seats lightly, then back it out about 1½ turns.

2. Start engine and warm it to normal operating temperature.

3. Turn idle speed screw until engine runs slower and begins to falter.

4. Adjust pilot air screw as required to make engine run smoothly.

5. Repeat Steps 3 and 4 to achieve the lowest stable idle speed.

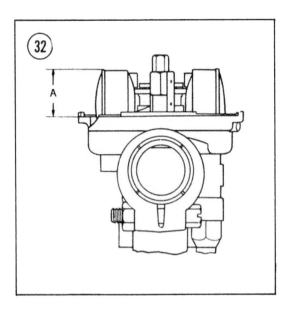

Component Section

Figure 34 illustrates those carburetor components which may be changed to meet individual operating conditions. Shown left to right

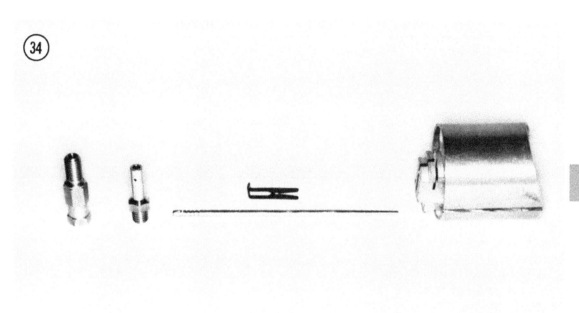

4

Condition	Symptom
Rich mixture	Rough idle
	Black exhaust smoke
	Hard starting, especially when hot
	"Blubbering" under acceleration
	Black deposits in exhaust pipe
	Gas-fouled spark plugs
	Poor gas mileage
	Engine performs worse as it warms up
Lean mixture	Backfiring
	Rough idle
	Overheating
	Hesitation upon acceleration
	Engine speed varies at fixed throttle
	Loss of power
	White color on spark plug insulator
	Poor acceleration

Next, determine proper throttle valve cutaway size. With the engine running at idle, open the throttle. If the engine does not accelerate smoothly from idle, turn the pilot air screw in (clockwise) slightly to richen the mixture. If the condition still exists, return the air screw to its original position and replace the throttle valve with one which has a smaller cutaway. If engine operation is worsened by turning the air screw, replace the throttle valve with one which has a larger cutaway.

For operation at ¼-¾ throttle opening, adjustment is made with the jet needle. Operate the engine at ½ throttle in a manner similar to that for full throttle tests described earlier. To richen the mixture, place the jet needle clip in a lower groove. Conversely, placing the clip in a higher groove leans the mixture.

A summary of carburetor adjustments is given in **Table 4**.

MISCELLANEOUS CARBURETOR PROBLEMS

Water in carburetor float bowls and sticking carburetor slide valves can result from careless washing of the motorcycle. To remedy the problem, remove and clean the carburetor bowl, main jet, and any other affected parts. Be sure to cover the air intake when washing the machine.

Be sure that the ring nut on top of the carburetor is neither too tight nor too loose. If the carburetor mounting cinch bolt is loose, the carburetor can pivot, resulting in an improper mixture because the float level is changed.

Table 4   CARBURETOR ADJUSTMENT SUMMARY

Throttle opening	Adjustment	If too rich	If too lean
0 - ⅛	Air screw	Turn out	Turn in
⅛ - ¼	Throttle valve cutaway	Use larger cutaway	Use smaller cutaway
¼ - ¾	Jet needle	Raise clip	Lower clip
¾ - full	Main jet	Use smaller number	Use larger number

If gasoline leaks past the float bowl gasket, high speed fuel starvation may occur. Varnish deposits on the outside of the float bowl are evidence of this condition.

Dirt in the fuel may lodge in the float valve and cause an overrich mixture. As a temporary measure, tap the carburetor lightly with any convenient tool to dislodge the dirt. Clean the fuel tank, petcock, fuel line, and carburetor at the first opportunity, should this occur. Check the starter plunger occasionally. The neoprene seal on the bottom may become damaged. If this should occur, fuel will leak into the chamber and eventually it will work its way into the carburetor venturi. This will cause the machine to run rich.

CHAPTER FIVE

ELECTRICAL SYSTEM

This chapter discusses operating principles and maintenance of the ignition, lighting, and charging systems.

FLYWHEEL MAGNETO OPERATION

A flywheel magneto provides electric power for the ignition and electrical systems of most of the models covered by this manual. Separate coils within the magneto supply current for ignition, daytime and nighttime operation, and battery charging. Alternating current produced by the magneto is used for ignition and lights, except for stoplights and turn signals. A rectifier converts this alternating current into direct current for charging the battery and operating the horn and turn signals. **Figure 1** illustrates construction of a typical magneto.

Figure 2 is a circuit diagram of a typical magneto ignition circuit. As the flywheel rotates, permanent magnets attached to the flywheel revolve past the various windings in the magneto, thereby inducing current in the windings.

When the contact breaker points are closed, the current (approximately 4 amperes) developed in the ignition coil is grounded, and no current is delivered to the ignition coil. When the points open, this current is delivered to the

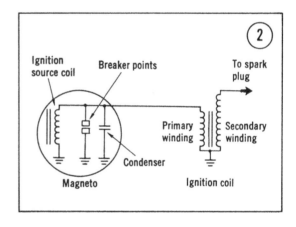

primary winding of the ignition coil. The 200 or 300 volts across the coil primary winding is stepped up to the very high voltage (10,000-15,000 volts) required to jump the spark plug gap. A capacitor (condenser) is connected across the breaker points. Action of the condenser assists the ignition coil in its task of developing the required high voltage, and also helps to prevent arcing and consequent burning of the breaker points.

Figure 3 illustrates a typical lighting and charging circuit. A portion of the current developed in the lighting coil is directed to the lighting circuits through the main switch; the remainder is used for charging the battery. The

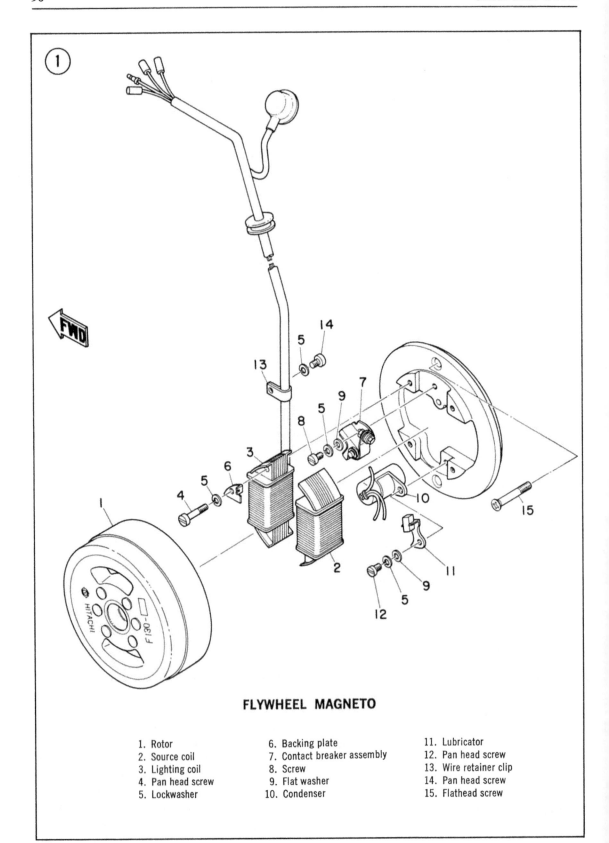

FLYWHEEL MAGNETO

1. Rotor
2. Source coil
3. Lighting coil
4. Pan head screw
5. Lockwasher
6. Backing plate
7. Contact breaker assembly
8. Screw
9. Flat washer
10. Condenser
11. Lubricator
12. Pan head screw
13. Wire retainer clip
14. Pan head screw
15. Flathead screw

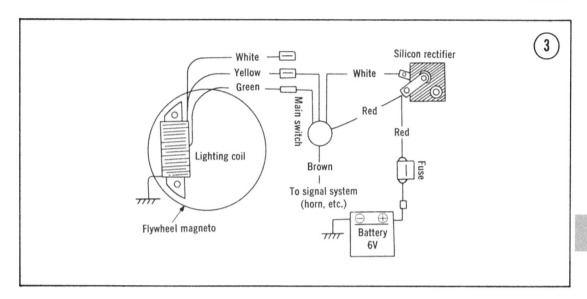

rectifier serves 2 purposes. It converts alternating current generated by the magneto into direct current for charging the battery, and it also prevents the battery from discharging through the magneto when magneto output voltage is too low to charge the battery.

Figures 4 and 5 are lighting and charging system diagrams for early and late model machines.

In cases where the battery is chronically undercharged, but otherwise in good condition, it is possible to increase its charging rate. Disconnect the green wire from the magneto where it connects to the green wire in the wiring harness. Then connect the red wire from the magneto to the green wire of the wiring harness.

MAGNETO TROUBLESHOOTING

In the event that an ignition malfunction is believed to be caused by a defective magneto on models with breaker points, check the coils, condenser, and breaker points as described in the following paragraphs.

Magneto Disassembly

A flywheel puller is required for this job. Do not attempt to remove the flywheel unless this tool is available.

1. Remove flywheel retaining nut, flat washer, and lockwasher. A tool is available to hold the flywheel while its retaining nut is loosened. If this tool is not available, a strap wrench works well. Another method is to feed a rolled-up rag between the primary reduction gears on the other side of the engine to prevent the crankshaft from turning.

2. Back out the screw fully from the flywheel puller body, then screw the puller fully into the flywheel center hole. Note that this hole has a left-hand thread.

3. Turn the puller screw clockwise to remove the flywheel (**Figure 6**).

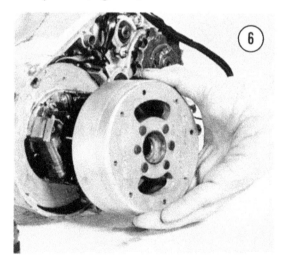

4. Remove the stator plate (**Figure 7**) after taking out its retaining screws.

5. Remove the Woodruff key from the crankshaft. To prevent this key from becoming lost,

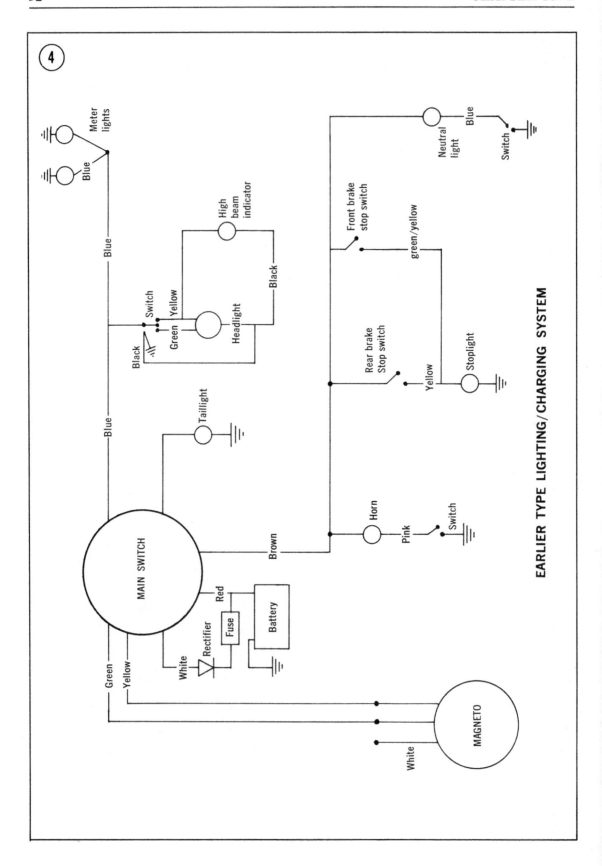

EARLIER TYPE LIGHTING/CHARGING SYSTEM

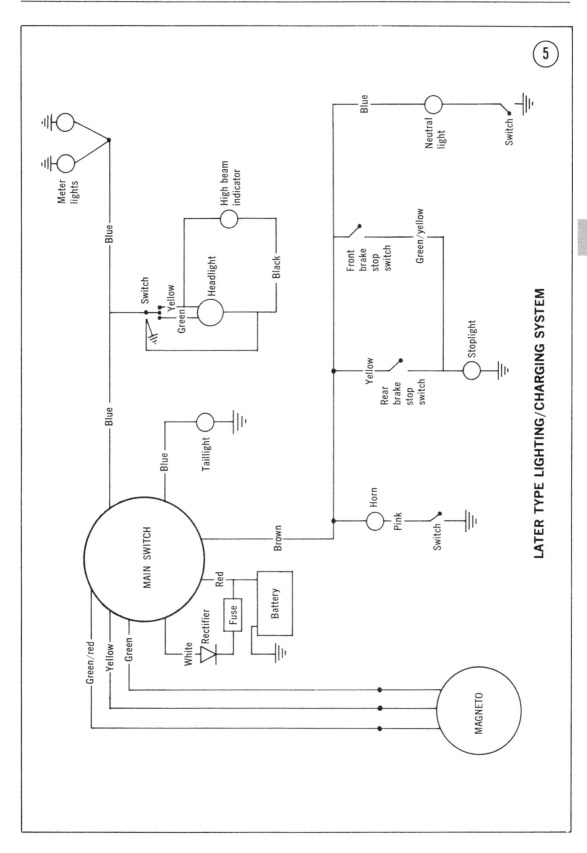

LATER TYPE LIGHTING/CHARGING SYSTEM

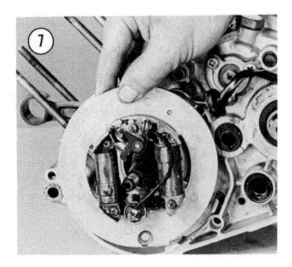

place it on one of the magnets inside the flywheel.

Reverse the foregoing procedure to install the magneto. Apply a very thin coating of distributor cam lubricant to the breaker cam inside the flywheel before installing the flywheel. Be sure that the Woodruff key is in place. Be sure to check ignition timing, and adjust it if necessary. Refer to Chapter Two for details.

Ignition Coil

With all magneto wiring disconnected, block the breaker points open with a piece of paper such as a business card.

Measure resistance between the movable breaker contact and ground with a low-range ohmmeter. If resistance is approximately 0.5 ohm, the coil is good.

If possible, disconnect the ground wire between the ignition coil and the magneto base. Measure insulation resistance between the iron core and the coil. Insulation resistance should be at least 5 megohms.

Condenser

Measure capacity of the condenser, using a condenser tester. Its capacity should be 0.18-0.25 mfd. With the condenser ground wire disconnected, measure insulation resistance between the outer case and the positive terminal. Insulation resistance should be over 5 megohms.

In the event that no test equipment is available, a quick test of the condenser may be made

by connecting the case to the negative terminal of a 6-volt battery, and the positive lead to the positive terminal. Allow the condenser to charge for a few seconds, then quickly disconnect the battery and touch the condenser lead to the case. If you observe a spark as the lead touches, you can assume that the condenser is good.

Arcing between the breaker points is a common symptom of a defective condenser.

Breaker Points

Refer to Chapter Two for details of breaker point service and ignition timing.

Lighting and Charging Coil

First be sure the battery is in good condition, then connect a 0-10 AC voltmeter between the yellow wire from the magneto and a good engine ground. Do not disconnect the yellow wire. Start the engine and turn on the lights. Run the engine at 2,500 rpm. The voltmeter must indicate at least 5.0 volts. Then increase engine speed to 8,000 rpm long enough to read the meter. The voltmeter must indicate no greater than 8.0 volts.

If the measurements obtained were not within specifications, check for poor connections or chafed wiring in the lighting and charging circuit. Refer back to Figure 4 or 5 as necessary to trace the circuits involved.

Charging Circuit Test (Early Models)

Before checking the charging system, be sure the battery is in good condition, and that it is fully charged. The following checks will not be meaningful if the battery is low or defective.

Connect the positive terminal of 0-10 DC voltmeter to the positive battery lead (red), and the negative voltmeter terminal to a good engine ground. Start the engine and run it under the conditions specified in **Table 1**.

Table 1   OUTPUT VOLTAGE

RPM	Voltage	Remarks
2,500	5.0 or greater	Lights on
8,000	8.0 or less	Lights on

With the engine not running, disconnect the red wire at the battery. Connect the positive terminal of a 0-5 DC ammeter to the wire which was disconnected. Connect the negative ammeter terminal to the positive battery terminal. Start the engine, then slowly increase rpm to 3,000. At this speed, the ammeter should show a slight charging current. Momentarily increase engine speed to 8,000 rpm. At that speed, charging current should not exceed 2.0 amperes.

If the charging system does not meet specifications, check all wiring, connections, magneto charging coil, main switch, and the rectifier.

Charging Circuit Test (Later Models)

Before checking the charging system, be sure that the battery is in good condition, and that it is fully charged. The following checks will not be meaningful if the battery is low or defective.

Connect the positive terminal of a 0-10 DC voltmeter to the positive battery lead (red), and the negative voltmeter terminal to a good engine ground. Start the engine and run it under the conditions listed in **Table 2**.

Table 2 CHARGING VOLTAGE

| RPM | Voltage | |
	Day	Night
2,000	8.0 ± 0.5	8.5 ± 0.5
8,000	8.5 ± 0.5	8.5 ± 0.5

With the engine not running, disconnect the red wire at the battery. Connect the positive terminal of a 0-5 DC ammeter to the wire which was disconnected. Connect the negative ammeter terminal to the positive battery terminal. Start the engine, then run it under each of the conditions listed in **Table 3**.

If the charging circuit does not meet specifications, check all wiring, charging coil, connections, main switch, and rectifier.

Rectifier

The rectifier serves 2 purposes. It converts alternating current produced by the magneto into direct current for charging the battery, and also prevents discharge of the battery through

Table 3 CHARGING CIRCUIT

| RPM | Voltage | |
	Day	Night
2,000	1.8 ± 0.5	0.7 ± 0.5
8,000	3.0 ± 0.5	1.5 ± 0.5

the magneto when the engine is not running, or at other times when magneto voltage is less than that of the battery.

To check the rectifier, measure its resistance in both forward and reverse directions. Resistance in one direction should be approximately 10 ohms. In the reverse direction, resistance should be essentially infinite (**Figure 8**). Never connect the rectifier directly to the battery to make a continuity check; doing so will cause instantaneous damage.

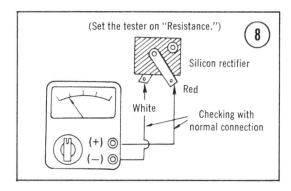

(Set the tester on "Resistance.") 8
Silicon rectifier
Red
White
Checking with normal connection
(+)
(−)

CAPACITOR DISCHARGE IGNITION (CDI)

A few models are equipped with electronic ignition. This solid state system, unlike conventional ignition systems, uses no breaker points or other moving parts. **Figure 9** illustrates system connections. **Figure 10** is an exploded view of the magneto used with this system.

No maintenance is required on the system other than that of making sure that all connecitons are clean and tight, and occasionally checking ignition timing. Refer to Chapter Two for ignition timing details.

STARTER/GENERATOR

Some models are equipped with a combination starter/generator (**Figure 11**). This unit

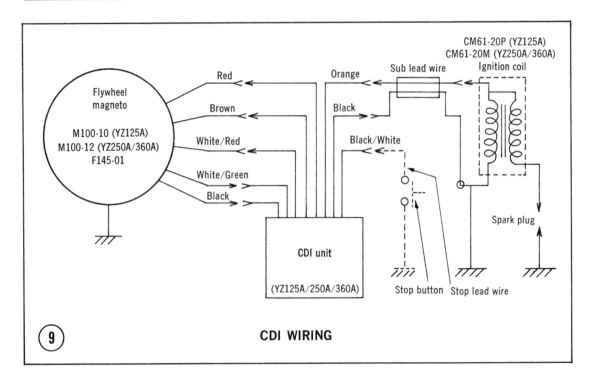

CDI WIRING

functions as a motor for engine starting, and as a generator when the engine is running. Also associated with this unit are the breaker points and ignition advance mechanism. **Figure 12** is a circuit diagram of a typical starter/generator system.

Checking Generator Output

To check output of the generator, proceed as follows.

1. Disconnect the white wire from terminal A.
2. Disconnect the green wire from terminal F.
3. Connect terminal E to terminal F with a jumper.
4. Connect the positive lead of a voltmeter to terminal A; connect the negative lead to ground.
5. Start the engine and run it at 1,800 rpm. Do not run the engine at a higher speed, as this will damage the coil and other electrical components.
6. If the voltmeter indicates 10 volts or more, the generator is in good condition.

Checking the Yoke

Before checking the yoke, clean it with a rag to remove carbon dust, oil, and other foreign material.

1. With the yoke removed, use an ohmmeter to be sure the positive brush is not shorted to ground.
2. Use the ohmmeter to determine continuity between terminals M and A, and between terminals A and F. If there is no continuity, and coil connections are good, replace the coil.
3. Poor brush condition is one of the most frequent causes of generator trouble. Remove the brushes and check them carefully. Each brush must contact the commutator with at least ¾ of its contact surface.

If brushes and commutator are rough, misalignment of the armature and crankshaft may be the cause. Check the tapered bore of the armature and smooth it if any burrs are found. If either brush is worn beyond the minimum length mark, replace both brushes. When you replace brushes, be sure that the positive brush lead does not touch the brush holder or the edge of the breaker plate. Also be sure the negative brush lead does not touch the positive brush spring.

Checking the Armature

1. Clean the armature of oil, dust, and foreign material.

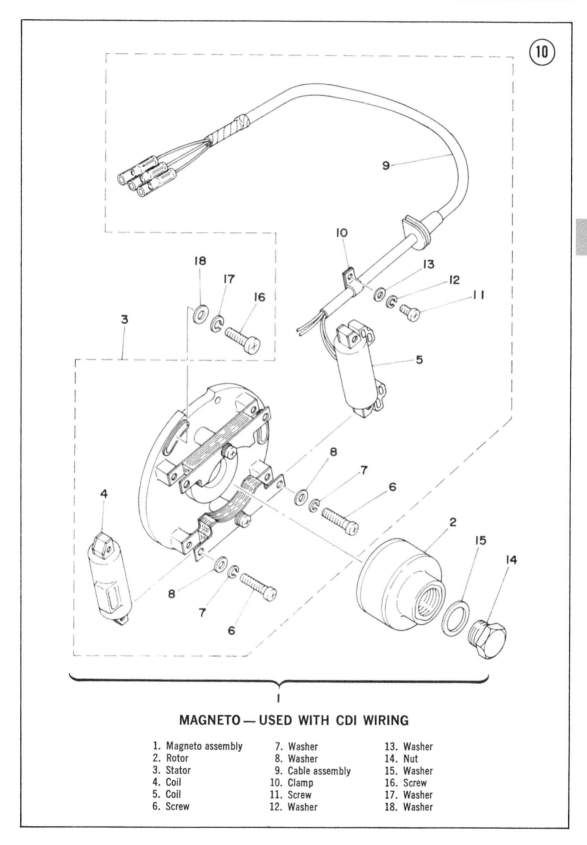

MAGNETO — USED WITH CDI WIRING

1. Magneto assembly	7. Washer	13. Washer
2. Rotor	8. Washer	14. Nut
3. Stator	9. Cable assembly	15. Washer
4. Coil	10. Clamp	16. Screw
5. Coil	11. Screw	17. Washer
6. Screw	12. Washer	18. Washer

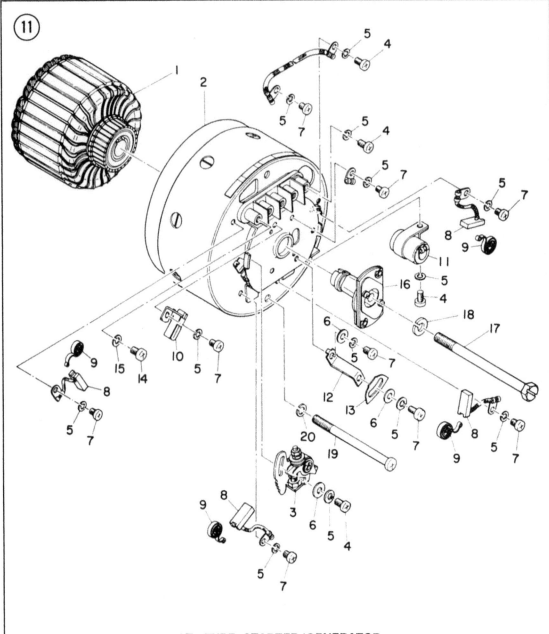

AT1-TYPE STARTER/GENERATOR

1. Armature
2. Stator assembly
3. Contact breaker assembly
4. Pan head screw
5. Spring washer
6. Washer
7. Pan head screw
8. Brush
9. Brush spring
10. Lubricator
11. Condenser
12. Timing plate fixture
13. Timing plate
14. Pan head screw
15. Spring washer
16. Governor assembly
17. Bolt
18. Spring washer
19. Stator screw
20. Spring washer

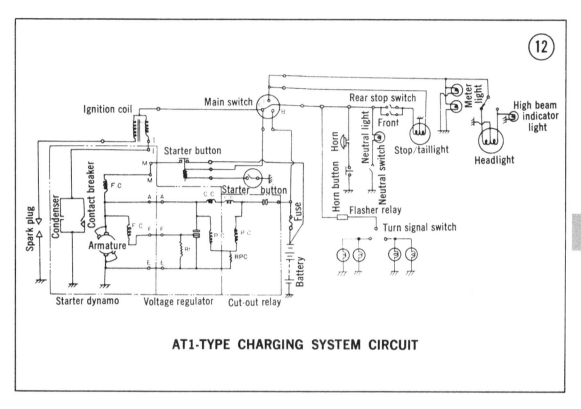

AT1-TYPE CHARGING SYSTEM CIRCUIT

2. If the commutator is only slightly rough, it may be polished with fine sandpaper.

If the commutator is out-of-round, burned, or too rough to polish, remove it, and turn it on a lathe. Do not turn it to a diameter of less than 1.5 in. (38mm).

3. If the commutator has high mica, undercut the mica segments with a broken hacksaw blade or mica undercutting tool. Be sure that there is no thin mica edge next to the commutator segments. The mica should be undercut 0.02-0.032 in. (0.5-0.8mm). See **Figure 13**.

4. Use an ohmmeter or armature growler to determine that no commutator segment is shorted to the shaft. If any short circuit exists, replace the armature.

Checking the Voltage Regulator

Varying engine speeds and electrical loads affect output voltage of the generator. The regulator controls output voltage, and also disconnects the battery from the generator whenever generator voltage is less than that of the battery, thereby preventing discharge of the battery through the generator.

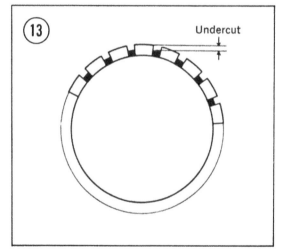

NOTE: *Do not attempt to make the following adjustments unless you have a voltmeter of known accuracy.*

To measure no-load voltage, disconnect the red wire from the regulator, then connect voltmeter probe to that wire. Ground the negative lead of the voltmeter. Start the engine and allow it to run at 2,500 rpm. **Figure 14** illustrates the connection. If the voltmeter does not indi-

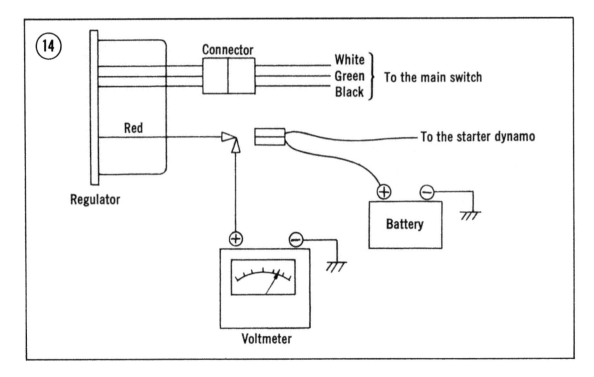

cate 15.8-16.5 volts, adjust the regulator output voltage with the adjustment screw on the regulator.

To measure cut-in voltage of the cutout relay, disconnect the wire from terminal A on the generator. Connect the positive lead of the voltmeter to terminal A; ground the negative lead. Start the engine, and slowly increase its speed as you observe the voltmeter. The cutout relay should close between 12.5 and 13.5 volts.

Under normal circumstances, the cutout relay will rarely, if ever, need adjustment. If its contacts are pitted or worn, dress them with fine emery cloth before adjustment.

Starter Troubleshooting

Table 4 lists symptoms, probable causes, and remedies for starter malfunctions.

Choke Coil

Some models are equipped with a choke coil in the night lighting circuit. As engine speed increases, so does output frequency of the lighting current developed in the magneto. Inductance of the choke coil tends to maintain current to the lights at a more constant level at high engine speed.

No maintenance is required on the choke coil. If its condition is doubtful, check it for continuity and insulation from ground.

LIGHTS

Machines designed to be ridden on public streets are equipped with lights. Check them periodically to be sure they are working.

Headlight

The headlight unit consists primarily of a lamp body, a dual-filament bulb, a lens and reflector unit, a rim, and a socket. To adjust the headlight, loosen the mounting bolts and move the assembly as required.

Turn Signals

If any turn signal bulb burns out, be sure to replace it with the same type. Improper action of the flasher relay, or even failure to operate may result from use of the wrong bulbs.

Brake Lights

The brake light switch is actuated by the brake pedal. Adjust the switch so that the stoplight goes on just before braking action occurs.

Table 4   STARTER TROUBLESHOOTING

Symptom	Probable Cause	Remedy
Starter does not work	Low battery	Recharge battery
	Worn brushes	Replace brushes
	Internal short	Repair or replace defective component
	Relay inoperative	Replace voltage regulator
	Defective wiring or connections	Repair wire or clean and tighten connections
	Defective switch	Replace switch
Starter action is weak	Low battery	Recharge battery
	Pitted relay contacts	Clean contacts or replace voltage regulator
	Brushes worn	Replace brushes
	Defective wiring or connections	Repair wire or clean and tighten connections
	Short in commutator	Replace armature
Starter runs continuously	Stuck relay	Dress contacts or replace voltage regulator

Move the switch body as required for adjustment. Tighten the clamp nut after adjustment.

HORN

Current for the horn is supplied by the battery. One horn terminal is connected to the battery through the main switch. The other terminal is connected to the horn button. When the rider presses the button, current flows through the horn.

Figure 15 illustrates horn construction. As current flows through the coil, the core becomes magnetized and attracts the armature. As the armature moves, it opens the contacts, cutting off the current. The diaphragm spring then returns the armature to its original position. This process repeats rapidly until the rider releases the horn button. Action of the armature striking the end of the core produces the sound, which is amplified by the resonator.

MAIN SWITCH

Service on the main switch is limited to checking continuity between the various circuits.

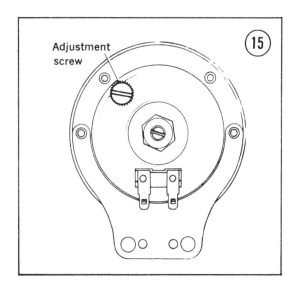

BATTERY

Most Yamaha bikes are equipped with lead-acid storage batteries, smaller in size but similar in construction to those found in automobiles.

WARNING
Read and thoroughly understand the section on Safety Precautions *before doing any battery service.*

Safety Precautions

When working with batteries, use extreme care to avoid spilling or splashing electrolyte. This electrolyte is sulphuric acid, which can destroy clothing and cause serious chemical burns. If any electrolyte is spilled or splashed on clothing or body, it should immediately be neutralized with a solution of baking soda and water, then flushed with plenty of clean water.

Electrolyte splashed into the eyes is extremely dangerous. Safety glasses should always be worn when working with batteries. If electrolyte is splashed into the eye, force the eye open, flood with cool clean water for about 5 minutes, and call a physician immediately.

If electrolyte is spilled or splashed onto painted or unpainted surfaces, it should be neutralized immediately with baking soda solution and then rinsed with clean water.

When batteries are being charged, highly explosive hydrogen gas forms in each cell. Some of this gas escapes through the filler openings and may form an explosive atmosphere around the battery. *This explosive atmosphere may exist for hours.* Sparks, open flame, or a lighted cigarette can ignite this gas, causing an internal explosion and possible serious personal injury. The following precautions should be taken to prevent an explosion.

1. Do not smoke or permit any open flame near any battery being charged or which has been recently charged.

2. Do not disconnect live circuits at battery terminals, because a spark usually occurs where a live circuit is broken. Care must always be taken when connecting or disconnecting any battery charger; be sure its power switch is off before making or breaking connections. Poor connections are a common cause of electrical arcs which cause explosions.

Electrolyte Level

Battery electrolyte level should be checked regularly, particularly during hot weather. Most batteries are marked with electrolyte level limit lines (**Figure 16**). Always maintain the fluid level between these lines, using distilled water as required for replenishment. Distilled water is

available at most supermarkets. It is sold for use in steam irons and is quite inexpensive.

Overfilling leads to loss of electrolyte, resulting in poor battery performance, short life, and excessive corrosion. Never allow the electrolyte level to drop below the top of the plates. That portion of the plates exposed to air may be permanently damaged, resulting in loss of battery performance and shortened life.

Excessive use of water is an indication that the battery is being overcharged. The most common causes of overcharging are high battery temperature or high voltage regulator setting. It is advisable to check the voltage regulator, on machines so equipped, if this situation exists.

Cleaning

Check the battery occasionally for presence of dirt or corrosion. The top of the battery, in particular, should be kept clean. Acid film and dirt permit current to flow between terminals, which will slowly discharge the battery.

For best results when cleaning, wash first with diluted ammonia or baking soda solution, then flush with plenty of clean water. Take care to keep filler plugs tight so that no cleaning solution enters the cells.

Battery Cables

To ensure good electrical contact, cables must be clean and tight on battery terminals. If the battery or cable terminals are corroded, the cables should be disconnected and cleaned separately with a wire brush and baking soda solution. After cleaning, apply a very thin coating of petroleum jelly to the battery terminals before installing the cables. After connecting the cables, apply a light coating to the connection. This procedure will help to prevent future corrosion.

Battery Charging

WARNING
Do not smoke or permit any open flame in any area where batteries are being charged, or immediately after charging. Highly explosive hydrogen gas is formed during the charging process. Be sure to reread Safety Precautions *in the beginning of this section.*

Motorcycle batteries are not designed for high charge or discharge rates. For this reason, it is recommended that a motorcycle battery be charged at a rate not exceeding 10 percent of its ampere-hour capacity. That is, do not exceed 0.5 ampere charging rate for a 5 ampere-hour battery. This charge rate should continue for 10 hours if the battery is completely discharged, or until specific gravity of each cell is up to 1.260-1.280, corrected for temperature. If after prolonged charging, specific gravity of one or more cells does not come up to at least 1.230, the battery will not perform as well as it should, but it may continue to provide satisfactory service for a time.

Some temperature rise is normal as a battery is being charged. Do not allow the electrolyte temperature to exceed 110°F. Should temperature reach that figure, discontinue charging until the battery cools, then resume charging at a lower rate.

Testing State of Charge

Although sophisticated battery testing devices are on the market, they are not available to the average motorcycle owner, and their use is be-

yond the scope of this book. A hydrometer, however, is an inexpensive tool, and will tell much about battery condition.

To use a hydrometer, place the suction tube into the filler opening and draw in just enough electrolyte to lift the float. Hold the instrument in a vertical position and read specific gravity on the scale, where the float stem emerges from the electrolyte (**Figure 17**).

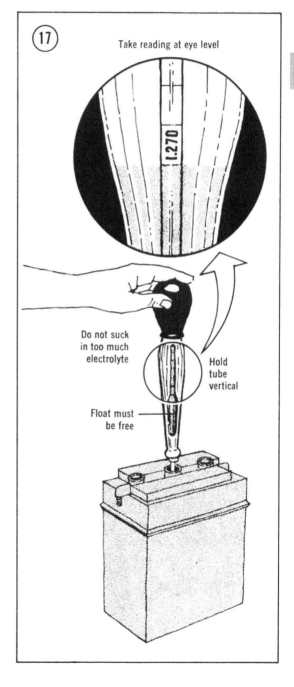

(17) Take reading at eye level

1.270

Do not suck in too much electrolyte

Hold tube vertical

Float must be free

Specific gravity of the electrolyte varies with temperature, so it is necessary to apply a temperature correction to the reading so obtained. For each 10 degrees that battery temperature exceeds 80°F, add 0.004 to the indicated specific gravity. Likewise, subtract 0.004 from the indicated value for each 10 degrees that battery temperature is below 80°F.

Repeat this measurement for each battery cell. If there is more than 0.050 difference (50 points) between cells, battery condition is questionable.

State of charge may be determined from **Table 5**.

Table 5   STATE OF CHARGE

Specific Gravity	State of Charge
1.110-1.130	Discharged
1.140-1.160	Almost discharged
1.170-1.190	One-quarter charged
1.200-1.220	One-half charged
1.230-1.250	Three-quarters charged
1.260-1.280	Fully charged

Do not measure specific gravity immediately after adding water. Ride the machine a few miles to ensure thorough mixing of the electrolyte.

It is most important to maintain batteries fully charged during cold weather. A fully charged battery freezes at a much lower temperature than does one which is partially discharged. Freezing temperature depends on specific gravity. See **Table 6**.

Table 6   BATTERY FREEZING TEMPERATURE

Specific Gravity	Freezing Temperature Degrees F
1.100	18
1.120	13
1.140	8
1.160	1
1.180	—6
1.200	—17
1.220	—31
1.240	—50
1.260	—75
1.280	—92

CHAPTER SIX

CHASSIS SERVICE

This chapter discusses service operations on wheels, brakes, suspension components, and related items. Chassis service is generally similar for all models; differences are pointed out where they exist.

WHEELS

Except for removal and installation, service on front and rear wheels is generally similar; differences are pointed out where they exist.

Front Wheel Removal

Figure 1 is an exploded view of a typical front wheel. Refer to that illustration during front wheel removal and service.

1. Support motorcycle so that front wheel is clear of ground. A box placed under the engine is a suitable support.
2. Disconnect brake cable at front brake lever (**Figure 2**).
3. Disconnect brake cable and speedometer cable at front wheel hub.
4. Loosen front axle pinch bolt (**Figure 3**), and cap bolts at lower end of the forks, if so equipped.
5. Remove axle nut (**Figure 4**).
6. Insert shank of a Phillips screwdriver into hole in axle, then simultaneously twist and pull the axle to remove it.

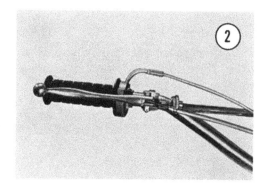

7. Roll wheel away from motorcycle. Be sure to catch any small parts, such as spacers, if they fall.

Front wheel installation is the reverse of removal. Be sure to tighten the axle pinch bolts and adjust the front brake.

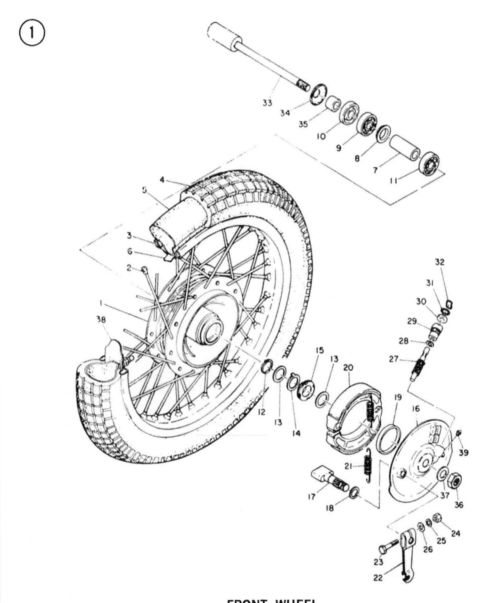

FRONT WHEEL

1. Hub	14. Meter clutch	27. Gear
2. Spoke	15. Drive gear	28. Thrust washer
3. Rim	16. Brake shoe plate	29. Bushing
4. Front tire	17. Cam	30. Oil seal
5. Tube	18. Camshaft shim	31. O-ring
6. Rim band	19. Oil seal	32. Stop ring
7. Spacer	20. Brake shoe	33. Axle
8. Spacer	21. Brake shoe return spring	34. Dust cover
9. Bearing	22. Camshaft lever	35. Spacer
10. Oil seal	23. Bolt	36. Shaft nut
11. Bearing	24. Nut	37. Spring washer
12. Snap ring	25. Spring washer	38. Rim lock
13. Thrust washer	26. Flat washer	39. Grease fitting

Rear Wheel Removal

Figures 5 and 6 are exploded views of typical rear wheels. Some models are equipped with rubber dampers in the rear hubs.

1. Support motorcycle so that rear wheel is clear of ground.

2. Remove brake rod and brake torque link from rear brake.

3. Loosen drive chain adjustment nuts on each side.

4. Remove rear axle nut.

5. Drive out rear axle, using a rawhide or plastic mallet.

6. Remove right-hand chain adjuster.

7. Remove rear brake plate.

8. Tilt motorcycle to the left, then roll rear wheel free.

Reverse the removal procedure to install the rear wheel. Be sure that all fasteners are tight, that the drive chain is adjusted, and that the rear brake is adjusted properly.

Spokes

Check spokes for tension. The "tuning fork" method for checking tension is simple and works well. Tap each spoke with a spoke wrench or screwdriver shank. A taut spoke will emit a clear, ringing tone; a loose spoke will sound flat. All spokes in a correctly tightened wheel will emit tones of similar pitch, but not necessarily the same tone.

Bent, stripped, or otherwise damaged spokes should be replaced as soon as they are detected. Unscrew the nipple from the spoke, then push the nipple far enough into the rim to free the end of the spoke, taking care not to push the spoke all the way in. Remove the defective spoke from the hub, then use it to match a new one of the same length. If necessary, trim the end of the new spoke slightly to match the original, then dress the threads. Install the new spoke, screw on the nipple, and tighten it until it emits a tone similar to that of the other spokes when it is struck. Check the new spoke periodically; it will stretch and so must be retightened several times until it takes its final set.

Spokes tend to loosen as the machine is used. Retighten each spoke one turn, beginning with those on one side of the hub, then those on the other side. Tighten the spokes on a new machine after the first 50 miles of operation, then at 50 mile intervals until they no longer loosen.

If the machine is subjected to particularly severe service, as in off-road or competition riding, check the spokes frequently.

Bead Protectors

Some machines are equipped with a bead protector (**Figure 7**) on each wheel. The bead protector prevents the tire from slipping on the rim, especially during maximum effort braking at high speed, and thereby prevents damage to the valve stem.

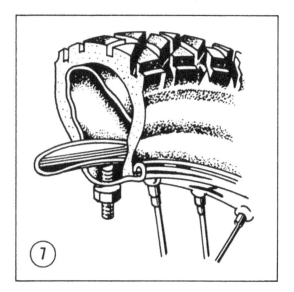

Rims

Check rims periodically for runout and out-of-round; also for bends or dents following a collision or hard spill. Severe rim damage is

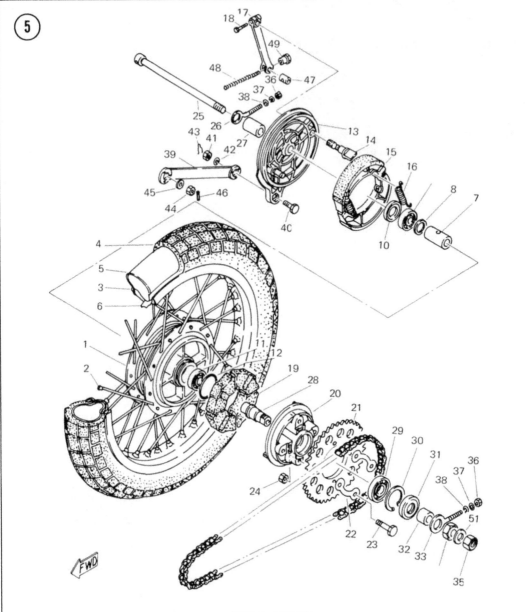

REAR WHEEL

1. Hub	13. Brake shoe plate	25. Axle	37. Lockwasher
2. Spoke	14. Camshaft	26. Chain puller (right)	38. Flat washer
3. Rim	15. Brake shoe	27. Axle collar	39. Tension bar
4. Tire	16. Return spring	28. Sprocket shaft	40. Tension bar bolt
5. Tube	17. Camshaft lever	29. Bearing	41. Nut
6. Rim band	18. Bolt	30. Circlip	42. Lockwasher
7. Bearing spacer	19. Clutch damper	31. Grease seal	43. Cotter pin
8. Spacer flange	20. Clutch hub	32. Sprocket shaft collar	44. Nut
9. Bearing	21. Sprocket	33. Chain adjuster (left)	45. Flat washer
10. Grease seal	22. Lockwasher	34. Sprocket shaft nut	46. Cotter pin
11. Bearing	23. Fitting bolt	35. Axle nut	47. Clevis pin
12. O-ring	24. Nut	36. Nut	48. Rod spring
			49. Nut

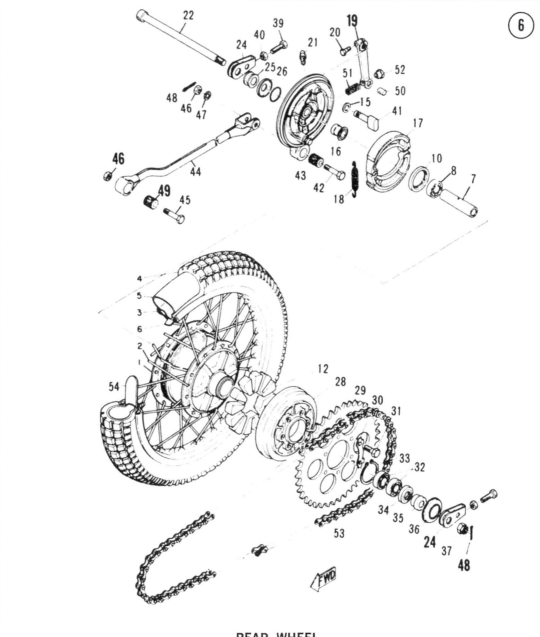

REAR WHEEL

1. Hub
2. Spoke
3. Rim
4. Tire
5. Tube
6. Rim band
7. Bearing spacer
8. Spacer flange
9. Bearing
10. Grease seal
11. O-ring
12. Clutch damper
13. Brake shoe plate
14. Cam
15. Camshaft shim
16. Shaft bushing
17. Brake shoe
18. Return spring
19. Camshaft lever
20. Bolt
21. Grease nipple
22. Axle
23. Axle collar
24. Chain adjuster
25. Axle collar
26. Dust cover plate
27. Sprocket shaft
28. Hub clutch
29. Sprocket
30. Lockwasher
31. Fitting bolt
32. Bearing
33. Circlip
34. Grease seal
35. Sprocket shaft collar
36. Dust cover
37. Axle nut
38. Shaft nut
39. Chain adjuster bolt
40. Nut
41. Blind plug
42. Pan head screw
43. Spring washer
44. Tension bar
45. Tension bar bolt
46. Nut
47. Lockwasher
48. Cotter pin
49. Tension bar clip
50. Clevis pin
51. Rod spring
52. Nut
53. Chain
54. Rim lock

difficult to repair successfully, and it is generally wiser and safer to replace the rim in such cases. The rubber rim band, which covers the spoke nipples and prevents them from chafing the inner tube, should be checked carefully each time the tire is removed. If the rim band is torn, exposing a spoke, replace or repair it with tape.

Wheel Balance

An unbalanced wheel results in unsafe riding conditions. Depending on the degree of unbalance and speed of the motorcycle, the rider may experience anything from a mild vibration to a violent shimmy which may even result in loss of control. Balance weights may be installed on spokes on the light side of the wheel to correct this condition.

Before attempting to balance wheels, check to be sure that the wheel bearings are in good condition and properly lubricated. Also make sure that brakes do not drag, so that wheels rotate freely. With the wheel free of the ground, spin it slowly and allow it to come to rest by itself. Add balance weights to the spokes on the light side as required, so that the wheel comes to rest at a different position each time it is spun. Balance weights are available in weights of 10, 20, and 30 grams. Remove the drive chain before balancing rear wheels.

If more than one ounce is required to balance the wheel, add weight to adjacent spokes; never put 2 or more weights on the same spoke. When the wheel comes to rest at a different point each time it is spun, consider it balanced and tightly crimp the weights so they will not be thrown off.

Checking Wheel Runout

To measure runout of the wheel rim, support the wheel so it is free to rotate. Position a dial indicator as shown in **Figure 8**. Observe the dial indicator as you rotate the wheel through a complete revolution. The runout limit for all models is 0.07 in. (2.0mm). Excessive runout may be caused by a bent rim or loose spokes. Repair or replace as required.

Miscellaneous Wheel Checks

1. Support each wheel shaft in a lathe, V-blocks, or other suitable centering device as

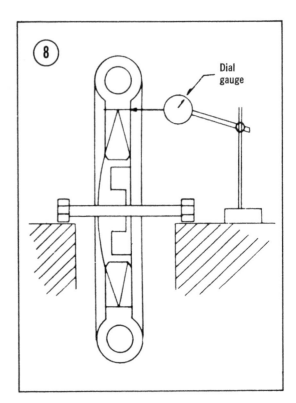

shown in **Figure 9**. Rotate the shaft through a complete revolution. Straighten or replace the shaft if it is bent more than 0.028 in. (0.7mm).

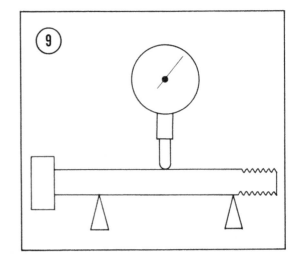

2. Check the inner and outer races of the wheel bearings for cracks, galling, or pitting. Rotate the bearings by hand and check for roughness. Replace the bearings if worn or damaged.

3. Inspect oil seals for wear or damage. Replace them if there is any doubt about their condition.

Removing Front Wheel Bearings

1. Clean dirt from wheel hub.

2. Make a bearing spacer removal tool, similar to that shown in **Figure 10**.

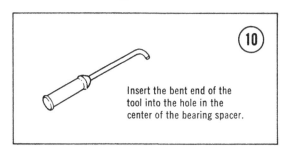

Insert the bent end of the tool into the hole in the center of the bearing spacer.

3. Refer to **Figure 11**. Place the bent end of the tool into the hole in the bearing spacer, then drive out the spacer and one bearing.

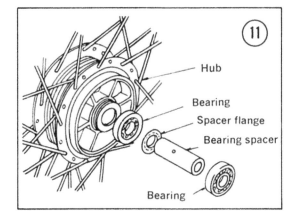

Hub
Bearing
Spacer flange
Bearing spacer
Bearing

4. Drive out the remaining bearing.

Reverse the removal procedure to install the front wheel bearings. Always clean and relubricate them whenever they are removed.

CAUTION
Be sure to install the spacer flange, on models so equipped. Failure to do so will result in premature bearing failure.

Replacing Clutch Hub Bearings

Figure 12 is an exploded view of a typical clutch hub on models with rear hub cushions. To replace bearings in such hubs, proceed as follows.

1. Push out sprocket shaft.

2. Pull out sprocket shaft spacer.

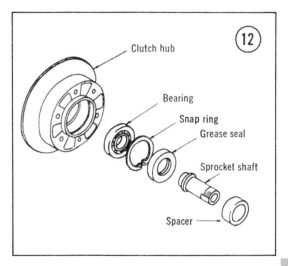

Clutch hub
Bearing
Snap ring
Grease seal
Sprocket shaft
Spacer

3. Remove grease seal.

4. Remove snap ring.

5. Press out bearing.

Reverse the removal procedure to install the bearing. Always install a new grease seal. Grease the bearing and grease seal lips upon assembly.

Rear Hub Cushions

Some models are equipped with rubber cushions in the rear hub. These cushions absorb sudden torque loads in the transmission, drive chain, and rear wheel. With use, they become worn and broken. Complete destruction is evidenced by a metallic "clunk" during acceleration or deceleration. Also, the hub will exhibit considerable angular free play. Perform the following procedure to inspect or replace the cushions.

1. Remove rear wheel.

2. Support rear wheel horizontally, with the sprocket upward.

3. Refer to **Figure 13**. Remove snap ring, then clutch hub, to expose cushions.

4. Inspect cushion cavities and snap ring groove in hub for cracks or other damage. Replace the hub in the event of damage.

Reverse the disassembly procedure to assemble the hub. Note that there are protrusions on the bottom of the clutch hub which fit into corresponding holes in each cushion. Replace the snap ring if it was distorted when removed.

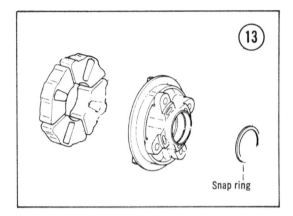

Snap ring

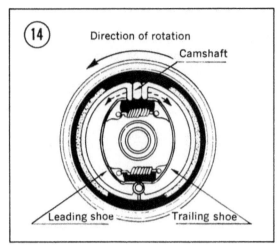

Direction of rotation
Camshaft
Leading shoe   Trailing shoe

On some models, the rubber cushions are permanently bonded to the clutch hub. When such cushions deteriorate, it is usually possible to tighten them and restore proper clutch hub operation. To do so, place shims, available at Yamaha dealers, under the snap ring which retains the clutch hub. If this procedure does not work, replace the clutch hub.

Rear Sprocket

To remove the sprocket on these models, place the wheel on a level surface with the sprocket upward. Using a blunt punch and a hammer, bend the tabs on the locking plate flat. Then remove the sprocket mounting bolts.

Check the bolts and lock plate for damage or breakage. If the tabs are not bent over the bolt, or are broken, or if the bolts are loose, the sprocket will loosen. Torque sprocket mounting bolts to 15 ft.-lb. (2.0 mkg). Be sure that all lock tabs are tight.

BRAKES

Each brake consists of a brake pedal or lever, cable or rod, brake shoe plate, and drum. The brake shoe plate assembly includes the brake cam, lever, brake shoes, retracting springs, and plate.

Brake Operation

Figure 14 illustrates typical brake operation. When the camshaft turns, it forces both shoes against the brake drum. Movement of the brake drum tends to increase the pressure of the forward shoe against the drum, therefore the

forward shoe is a leading shoe because of this self-energizing effect. The rear shoe, however, makes contact in the direction of the drum rotation, and the self-energizing effect does not occur. Therefore, the rear brake shoe is a trailing shoe.

Brake Inspection

Measure outer diameter of the brake shoe assembly, as shown in **Figure 15**. Wear limits for the various models are listed in **Table 1**.

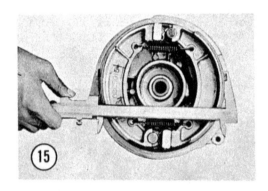

Examine inner surfaces of the brake drums for cracks, grooves, or other damage. Any groove deep enough to catch a fingernail is cause to consider brake drum replacement.

Replace oil-soaked brake shoes immediately.

Replacing Brake Shoes

Place the brake shoe plate on a firm, flat surface, with the brake shoes upward, then proceed as follows.

Table 1   BRAKE WEAR SPECIFICATIONS

Model	Standard Size		Wear Limit	
	Inches	(mm)	Inches	(mm)
YZ80A	3.74	(95)	3.54	(90)
80	4.33	(110)	4.09	(104)
90	4.33	(110)	4.09	(104)
100	4.33	(110)	4.09	(104)
YZ100C	5.12	(130)	4.92	(125)
125	4.33	(110)	4.09	(104)
DT125 A	5.12	(130)	4.92	(125)
175	4.33	(110)	4.09	(104)
DT175 A	5.12	(130)	4.92	(125)

1. Hold one shoe securely, then carefully lift the other shoe until it pivots away from the anchor and pivot at its ends. Be careful; the return springs are under considerable tension.

2. Unhook both return springs.

3. Remove remaining shoe.

4. Place both new shoes on a flat surface, then install both return springs.

5. Place one shoe in position, with its flat end against the brake cam, and its radiused end against the stationary anchor pin.

6. Hold the shoe installed in Step 5, then slip the ends of the remaining shoe over the anchor pin and cam. Finally, press the shoe into position against the brake shoe plate (**Figure 16**).

7. Turn the cam slightly, and apply grease sparingly to the contact surfaces (**Figure 17**).

Adjusting Front Brake

Refer to **Figure 18**. Loosen locknut (A), then turn cable adjuster (B) to provide 0.2-0.3 in.

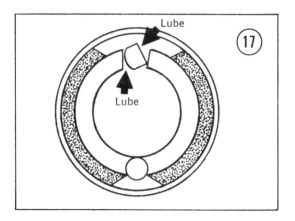

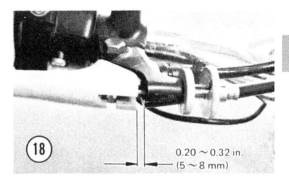

(5-8mm) clearance to the mounting bracket when all cable slack is taken up.

Some models are equipped with an additional adjuster at the front wheel. Use it as needed.

Rear Brake Adjustment

Proper rear brake adjustment results when there is approximately one inch (25mm) brake pedal travel before the rear brake starts to take effect. **Figure 19** illustrates the rear brake adjustment nut. Turn it in or out as required.

NOTE: *There is no locknut. Be sure that the special spring is in place on the rod, just forward of the rear brake lever.*

Rear Brake Modification

Rear brake action may be too sensitive for some riders. If the rear wheel locks, and skidding results, try the following procedure.

1. Bend the rod which connects the brake pedal and rear brake lever until it has a definite and permanent bow. This procedure is usually enough to decrease rear brake sensitivity; but if not, continue with Step 2.

2. Remove both brake shoes. Mark them so that they may be returned to their original locations.

3. Carefully clamp each brake shoe in a vise, then file grooves at an angle across the friction surfaces (**Figure 20**). These grooves should be approximately ¼ in. (6mm) wide, and no deeper than ½ the thickness of the lining. Slightly chamfer the edge of the grooves which contact the brake drum.

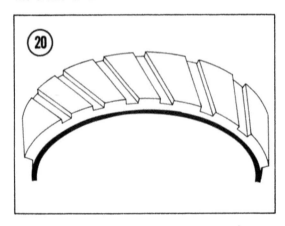

To start, space the grooves about 2 in. (5cm) apart, then reassemble the brake and test its response. Add additional grooves between the original ones if necessary.

FRONT FORK

All models are equipped with an oil-damped telescopic front fork. **Figures 21, 22 and 23** are exploded views of typical forks on these models. Refer to the applicable illustration during fork removal and service.

Fork Removal

Fork removal is generally similar for all models.

1. Support front of motorcycle so that front wheel is clear of ground.

2. Remove front wheel.

3. Remove front fender and fork brace.

4. Remove tachometer and speedometer, if so equipped.

5. Refer to **Figure 24**. Loosen pinch bolts (A), then remove fork cap bolts (B).

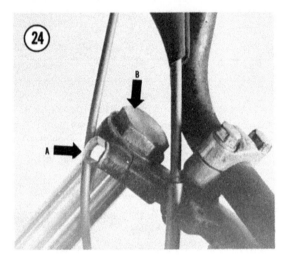

WARNING
This cap bolt is under considerable spring pressure. Hold it to prevent it from flying off and causing possible injury.

6. Refer to **Figure 25**. Loosen pinch bolts (C).

7. Support headlight assembly, if so equipped, then pull fork tube downward to remove it from steering head.

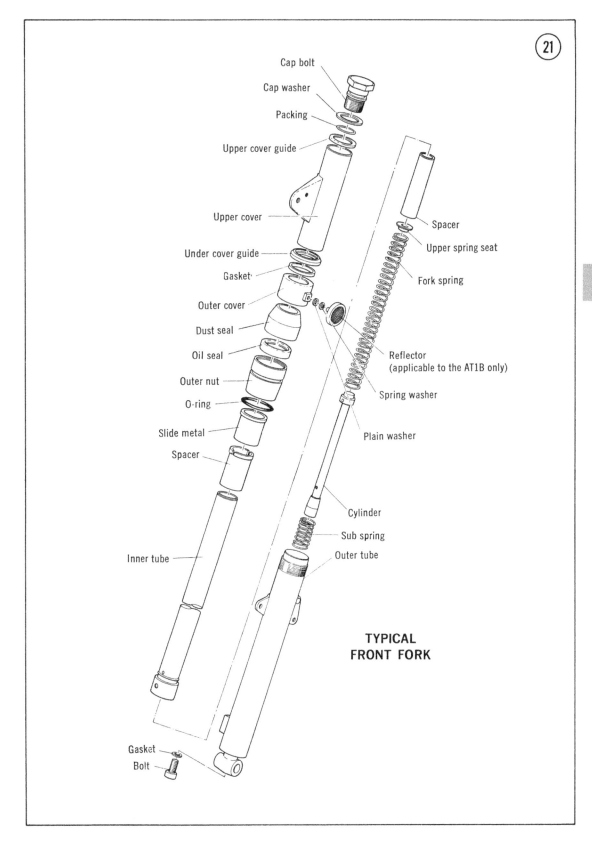

Cap bolt
Cap washer
Packing
Upper cover guide
Upper cover
Under cover guide
Gasket
Outer cover
Dust seal
Oil seal
Outer nut
O-ring
Slide metal
Spacer
Inner tube
Gasket
Bolt

Spacer
Upper spring seat
Fork spring
Reflector
(applicable to the AT1B only)
Spring washer
Plain washer
Cylinder
Sub spring
Outer tube

**TYPICAL
FRONT FORK**

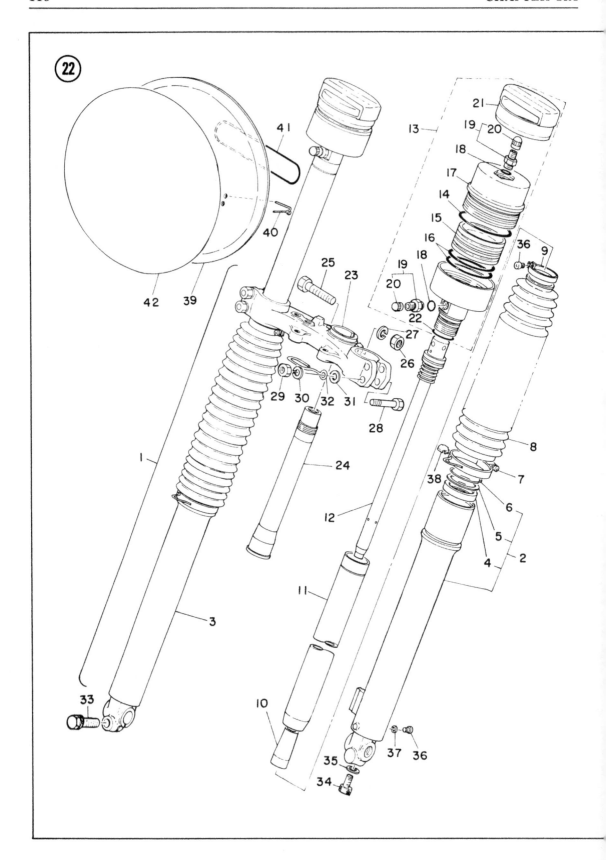

TYPICAL
FRONT FORK

1. Fork assembly
2. Tube
3. Tube
4. Oil seal
5. Washer
6. Snap ring
7. Cable retainer
8. Boot
9. Boot band
10. Spindle
11. Tube
12. Cylinder
13. Chamber assembly
14. O-ring
15. Piston
16. O-ring
17. Cap
18. O-ring
19. Valve
20. Valve cap
21. Cap
22. O-ring
23. Underbracket
24. Shaft
25. Bolt
26. Nut
27. Washer
28. Bolt
29. Nut
30. Washer
31. Washer
32. Cable retainer
33. Bolt
34. Bolt
35. Packing
36. Drain plug
37. Gasket
38. Retainer
39. Number plate
40. Brace
41. O-ring
42. Emblem

Fork Tube Disassembly

1. Obtain a suitable drain pan, then invert fork leg to drain its oil. Note that the spacer, upper spring seat, and spring will fall out at this time.

2. On all but 80cc and 90cc models, remove Allen bolt from outer fork tube (**Figure 26**).

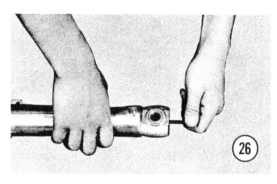

3. Refer back to Figure 21. On models with an outer nut (left center of illustration), continue with Step 4. On models without this nut, pull fork tubes apart.

4. Wrap a piece of old inner tube or similar rubber sheet around outer tube nut, then clamp it in a vise. Turn outer tube counterclockwise to remove nut and separate tubes.

5. Remove damper unit (**Figure 27**). On some models, the damper unit is retained by a snap ring, which must be removed first.

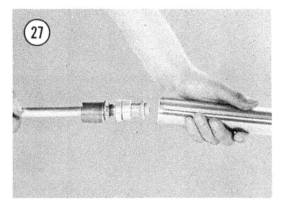

Fork Inspection

Check inner fork tubes for bends or scratches. Slightly bent tubes may be straightened. Any rust or corrosion on the inner fork tube in the area where it passes through the oil seal is cause for replacement.

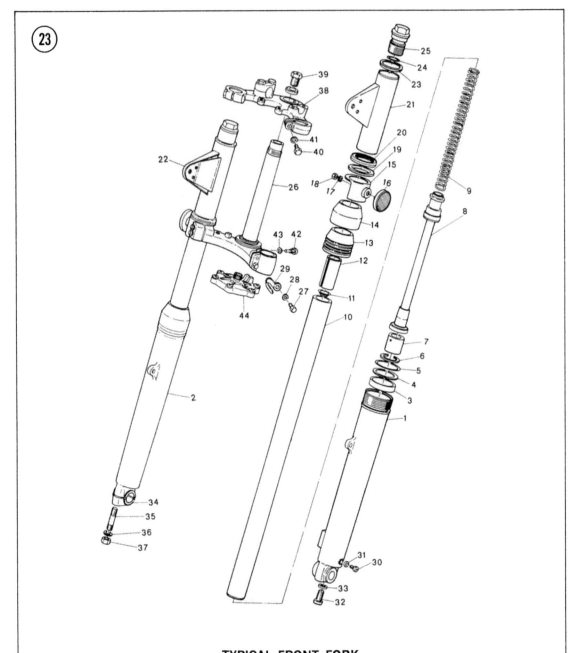

TYPICAL FRONT FORK

1. Left outer tube	12. Spacer	23. Upper cover guide	34. Axle retainer
2. Right outer tube	13. Dust seal	24. Gasket	35. Axle retainer bolt
3. Oil seal	14. Dust seal cover	25. Cap bolt	36. Lockwasher
4. Oil seal washer	15. Outer cover	26. Underbracket	37. Nut
5. Oil seal snap ring	16. Reflector	27. Underbracket bolt	38. Handle crown
6. Circlip	17. Lockwasher	28. Lockwasher	39. Underbracket retaining bolt
7. Piston	18. Nut	29. Cable holder	40. Bolt
8. Cylinder	19. Gasket	30. Drain screw	41. Lockwasher
9. Spring	20. Lower cover guide	31. Drain screw gasket	42. Bolt
10. Inner tube	21. Left cover	32. Bolt	43. Lockwasher
11. Upper spring seat	22. Right cover	33. Gasket	44. Steering damper unit

Compare overall spring length with that of new springs. If they are shorter than new ones by ¼ in. (6mm), replace both springs.

Seepage past the oil seal indicates need for oil seal replacement.

Oil Seal Replacement

On models with a ring nut which holds both fork tubes together, the oil seal is located inside the ring nut; on other models, the oil seal is located inside the outer tube.

1. Pry out snap ring, washer, and dust seal.

2. Refer to **Figure 28**. Carefully pry out oil seal, using a folded rag to protect the outer tube.

3. Position new seal with its open end downward, then gently tap all around its exposed surface to start it into position. Once it is started, use a socket wrench of appropriate diameter as a seal driver and a light hammer to seal it.

4. Install dust seal, washer, and snap ring.

5. Lubricate oil seal lip.

6. Assemble fork leg.

Fork Reassembly

1. To assemble the front fork, reverse the disassembly procedure. Be sure that the inner tube slides in and out smoothly. Always replace the oil seal under outer tube nut upon reassembly.

2. To install the front fork on the frame, place each tube assembly in the correct position. Tighten both lower pinch bolts just enough to prevent the fork tube from falling, then add fork oil. Install and tighten the cap bolt completely. Then tighten both lower and upper pinch bolts.

NOTE: *Refill each fork leg with 10W-30 motor oil through the opening in the upper end. The correct oil quantity is listed in* **Table 2.**

Table 2   FORK OIL QUANTITY

Model	Ounces	Milliliters
YZ80	3.6-3.7	105-110
80	Lt 3.25 Rt 4.1	Lt 96 Rt 120
90	4.5-5.0	132-147
100	4.6	135
YZ100 C	6.4	191
MX100A	6.3	187
DT100 A	5.4	160
AT1 series	4.9-5.4	145-160
AT2, AT3 series	4.1	120
DT, MX, YZ125	4.4	130
CT1 series	4.9-5.4	145-160
CT2, CT3	4.1	120
DT, MX175 A	7.1	210

Fork Oil Change

Water, dust, and aluminum particles gradually contaminate the fork oil. For this reason, fork oil should be changed every 4,000 miles (6,000 km) on models used for street riding, and much more frequently on those models used for off-road riding.

1. Place a suitable collection vessel under each fork leg.

2. Remove fork oil drain screws (**Figure 29**).

3. Lock front brake, then pump forks up and down until all oil drains.

4. Replace drain screws. Be careful; it is easy to cross-thread these screws.

5. Loosen upper pinch bolts (A, Figure 24), then remove fork cap bolts.

WARNING
Fork cap bolts are under considerable spring pressure. Hold them firmly to prevent them from flying away and causing possible injury.

6. Fill each fork leg with the correct amount of fork oil specified in foregoing Table 2.

7. Lock front brake, then pump forks up and down gently until all oil has drained into the lower portion of each fork leg.

8. Install fork cap bolts, then tighten upper pinch bolts.

STEERING HEAD

Figures 30 and 31 are exploded views of typical steering heads. Refer to the appropriate illustration during steering head disassembly and service.

Check steering head bearing races and balls occasionally for pitting, cracks, or wear. If any of these conditions exist, replace all balls and races. Never use any combination of new and used parts.

1. Disconnect clutch cable, throttle cable, and front brake cable at handlebar.

2. Remove headlight, if so equipped, and disconnect any wiring to switches on handlebar.

3. Remove handlebar.

4. Remove speedometer and tachometer, if so equipped.

5. Remove front wheel.

6. Remove both front fork legs.

7. Remove steering damper, if so equipped.

8. Remove bolt from center of upper bracket, then remove upper bracket.

9. Remove ring nut (12, Figure 31). This nut may be started by tapping it counterclockwise with a small hammer and punch. Hold lower bracket to prevent it from dropping and balls from falling out.

10. Remove race cover, upper race, and all upper balls. Note that there are 22 small balls

in the upper bearing. A small magnet may be helpful during this step.

11. Lower the underbracket slightly, then remove 19 lower balls. Hold a rag under the work area to catch any balls that may drop.

12. Tap out inner races, if necessary, with a long drift and small hammer.

13. To remove the lowermost race, carefully wedge it up over the underbracket stem.

Steering head assembly is the reverse of disassembly. Observe the following notes.

1. Tap races in carefully until they are fully seated.

2. Apply heavy grease to the lowermost race (on underbracket stem) to hold balls in position, then install all 19 balls. Apply more grease after balls are in position.

3. Hold underbracket in position, grease upper bearing race liberally, install 22 small balls, then apply more grease.

4. Complete reassembly in reverse order of disassembly.

To adjust steering head bearing, proceed as follows.

1. Using a hammer and suitable drift, tighten ring nut until fork turns from one limit to the other, with no binding or looseness.

2. Install all remaining parts, then again check the adjustment.

REAR SUSPENSION

On most models, the rear suspension consists of a swinging arm assembly, 3-position adjustable springs, and shock absorbers. On some models, a single Monocross shock absorber is combined with a swinging arm. **Figure 32** is an exploded view of a typical rear suspension system with dual shock absorbers. **Figure 33** illustrates Yamaha's Monocross suspension.

Shock Absorbers

To check shock absorbers, remove one of them from the motorcycle by unbolting its retaining hardware. Leave the remaining unit in place. Then proceed as follows.

1. Press upper end of spring downward, remove both half-moon keepers, then remove spring.

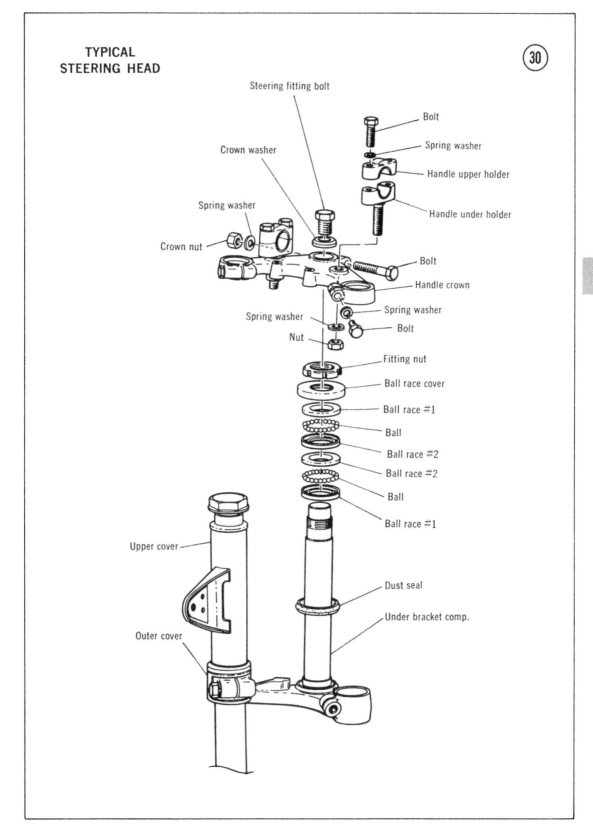

**TYPICAL
STEERING HEAD**

(30)

Steering fitting bolt

Bolt

Crown washer

Spring washer

Handle upper holder

Handle under holder

Spring washer

Crown nut

Bolt

Handle crown

Spring washer

Spring washer

Bolt

Nut

Fitting nut

Ball race cover

Ball race #1

Ball

Ball race #2

Ball race #2

Ball

Ball race #1

Upper cover

Dust seal

Under bracket comp.

Outer cover

6

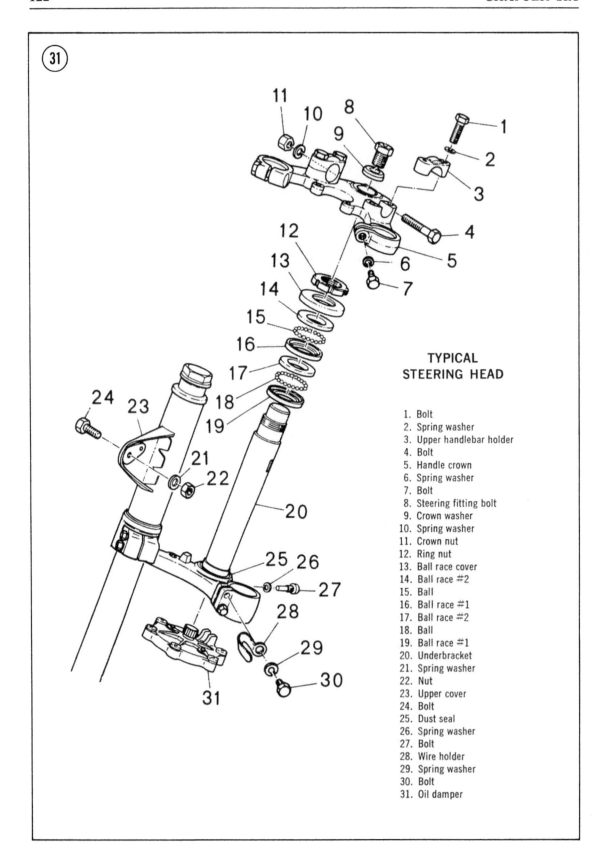

TYPICAL
STEERING HEAD

1. Bolt
2. Spring washer
3. Upper handlebar holder
4. Bolt
5. Handle crown
6. Spring washer
7. Bolt
8. Steering fitting bolt
9. Crown washer
10. Spring washer
11. Crown nut
12. Ring nut
13. Ball race cover
14. Ball race #2
15. Ball
16. Ball race #1
17. Ball race #2
18. Ball
19. Ball race #1
20. Underbracket
21. Spring washer
22. Nut
23. Upper cover
24. Bolt
25. Dust seal
26. Spring washer
27. Bolt
28. Wire holder
29. Spring washer
30. Bolt
31. Oil damper

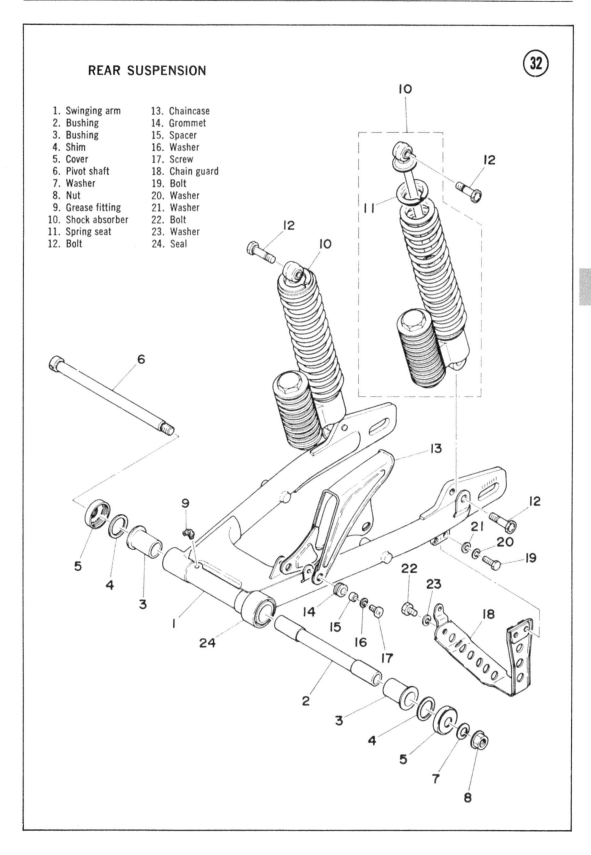

REAR SUSPENSION

1. Swinging arm
2. Bushing
3. Bushing
4. Shim
5. Cover
6. Pivot shaft
7. Washer
8. Nut
9. Grease fitting
10. Shock absorber
11. Spring seat
12. Bolt

13. Chaincase
14. Grommet
15. Spacer
16. Washer
17. Screw
18. Chain guard
19. Bolt
20. Washer
21. Washer
22. Bolt
23. Washer
24. Seal

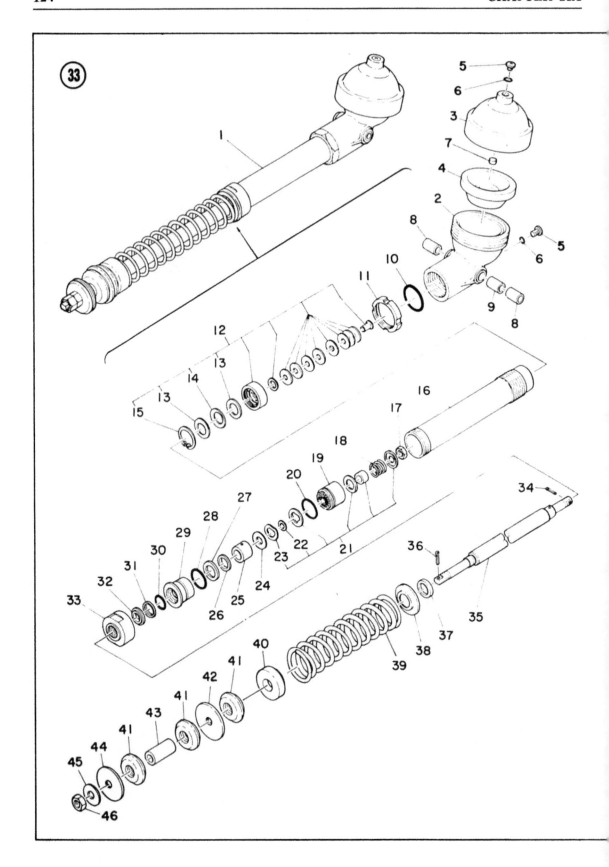

MONOCROSS
REAR SUSPENSION

1. Monocross assembly
2. Diaphragm housing
3. Cap
4. Diaphragm
5. Screw
6. O-ring
7. Valve
8. Bushing
9. Spacer
10. O-ring
11. Ring nut
12. Base valve set
13. Plate
14. Spring
15. Snap ring
16. Cylinder
17. Nut
18. Spring
19. Piston
20. O-ring
21. Piston valve set
22. Plate
23. Spring
24. Washer
25. Stopper
26. Spacer
27. Damper
28. O-ring
29. Seal ring housing
30. O-ring
31. O-ring
32. Oil seal
33. Cap
34. Cotter pin
35. Piston rod
36. Cotter pin
37. Washer
38. Spring guide
39. Spring
40. Spring seat
41. Damper
42. Nut plate
43. Spacer
44. Washer
45. Washer
46. Nut

2. Extend shock absorber shaft fully.

3. Push shaft in quickly. It should go in with little resistance.

4. Push shaft in fully.

5. Try to pull shaft out quickly. The shock absorber shaft must slide out slowly, no matter how hard it is pulled. Replace the shock absorber if the shaft pulls out easily.

6. Assemble spring and shock absorber, then install assembly on motorcycle.

7. Remove remaining shock absorber, then repeat Steps 1 through 6.

WARNING
Monocross shock absorbers contain nitrogen gas under high pressure. Use only nitrogen when refilling the suspension unit. Do not attempt to disassemble the suspension unit. Do not incinerate discarded Monocross suspension units.

To remove the Monocross unit, proceed as follows.

1. Turn fuel petcock off, then remove fuel tank.

2. Remove both pivot shaft nuts. Upon installation, tighten these nuts to 51 ft.-lb. (9.0 mkg). Remove washer and bushing.

3. Remove bolt which secures diaphragm housing to rear of frame. Take care not to lose its washer. Upon installation, tighten nut to 14.5 ft.-lb. (2.0 mkg).

4. Lift swinging arm, then pull out suspension unit from rear.

Reverse the removal procedure to install the suspension unit.

A few items on the Monocross suspension system require periodic inspection. Refer to **Figure 34.**

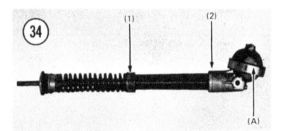

1. Remove spring.

2. Loosen ring nut (2).

3. Tighten case cap (1) to 108 ft.-lb. (15 mkg).

4. Retighten ring nut (2) to 146 ft.-lb. (20 mkg).

It is possible to install suspension unit springs with different characteristics. Soft, standard, and hard springs are avaiable. To replace this spring, proceed as follows.

1. Remove Monocross suspension unit.

2. Cover diaphragm housing bolt holes with rags, then clamp unit in a vise.

3. Remove spring retaining nut and its related hardware.

4. Lift off spring.

Reverse the removal procedure to install the new spring. Upon installation, tighten its nut to 11 ft.-lb. (1.5 mkg).

Swinging Arm

Occasionally check for play in swinging arm bushings. To do so, remove the rear wheel and both shock absorbers or Monocross suspension unit. Then shake the swinging arm from side to side. If there is noticeable play, replace the swing arm bushings and/or shaft. On models used primarily for street riding, these bushings should be replaced at 6,000 mile (10,000 km) intervals. Models used for competition will require replacement at more frequent intervals. Need for replacement may be indicated by shimmy, wander, or rear wheel hop.

1. Remove chaincase mounting bolts.

2. Remove shaft nut, then pull out shaft.

3. Remove old bushings.

Reverse the removal procedure to install new bushings.

DRIVE CHAIN

The drive chain is subject to wear and abrasion, and as such, it must be cleaned frequently, lubricated, and adjusted if it is to provide long service.

Cleaning and Lubrication

1. Disconnect master link, then remove chain from motorcycle.

2. Immerse chain in cleaning solvent, and allow it to soak for about ½ hour. Move it around and flex it during this period so that dirt between pins and rollers can work its way out.

3. Scrub rollers and side plates with a stiff brush, then rinse chain in clean solvent to carry away loosened dirt. Hang chain and allow to dry thoroughly.

4. Lubricate chain with a good grade of chain lubricant, carefully following the lubricant manufacturer's instructions.

5. Reinstall chain on motorcycle. Use a new master link clip and install it in the direction shown in **Figure 35**.

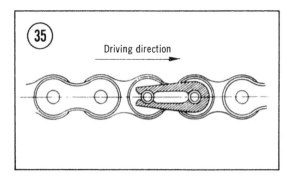

Chain Inspection

1. Refer to **Figure 36**. Replace the chain if it can be pulled away from the rear sprocket more than ½ the length of a link.

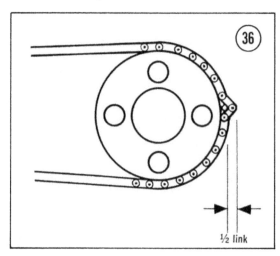

2. Check for binding links. To do so, hang the chain by one end. If there are any binding links, the chain will exhibit a kink at that point. If

cleaning and lubrication does not help the problem, replace the chain.

3. Rust results in rapid wear of pins and rollers. If rust is present, clean and lubricate the chain at once.

Chain Adjustment

When the drive chain is properly adjusted, vertical play in the lower chain run will be approximately ¾-1 in. (20-25mm). If adjustment is required, proceed as follows.

1. Loosen rear axle locknut. On models with rubber rear hub dampers, there is an additional nut which must be loosened.

2. Loosen both chain adjuster locknuts, then turn both chain adjusters as required to adjust chain free play.

3. Refer to **Figure 37**. Note that there is an alignment mark on each chain adjuster, and several marks on each swing arm. The alignment mark on each chain adjuster must align with corresponding swing arm marks. For example, if the left chain adjuster aligns with the third swing arm mark from the front, the right chain adjuster must align with the third mark from the front. Turn either adjuster as required until this condition exists.

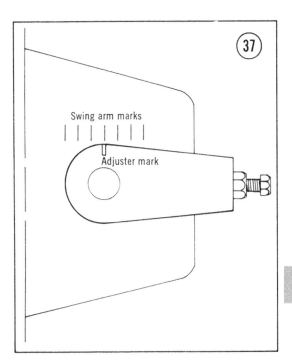

4. Recheck chain free play, and readjust if required by turning both chain adjusters an equal amount.

5. Tighten axle nut and chain adjuster locknuts.

6. Chain adjustment may affect rear brake adjustment. Adjust the rear brake if necessary.

CHAPTER SEVEN

TROUBLESHOOTING

Diagnosing motorcycle ills is relatively simple if you use orderly procedures and keep a few basic principles in mind.

Never assume anything. Don't overlook the obvious. If you are riding along and the bike suddenly quits, check the easiest, most accessible problem spots first. Is there gasoline in the tank? Is the gas petcock in the ON or RESERVE position? Has the spark plug wire fallen off? Check the ignition switch. Sometimes the weight of keys on a key ring may turn the ignition off suddenly.

If nothing obvious turns up in a cursory check, look a little further. Learning to recognize and describe symptoms will make repairs easier for you or a mechanic at the shop. Describe problems accurately and fully. Saying that "it won't run" isn't the same as saying "it quit on the highway at high speed and wouldn't start", or that "it sat in my garage for three months and then wouldn't start".

Gather as many symptoms together as possible to aid in diagnosis. Note whether the engine lost power gradually or all at once, what color smoke (if any) came from the exhaust, and so on. Remember that the more complicated a machine is, the easier it is to troubleshoot because symptoms point to specific problems.

You don't need fancy equipment or complicated test gear to determine whether repairs can be attempted at home. A few simple checks could save a large repair bill and time lost while the bike sits in a dealer's service department. On the other hand, be realistic and don't attempt repairs beyond your abilities. Service departments tend to charge heavily for putting together a disassembled engine that may have been abused. Some won't even take on such a job— so use common sense; don't get in over your head.

OPERATING REQUIREMENTS

An engine needs 3 basics to run properly: correct gas/air mixture, compression, and a spark at the right time. If one or more are missing, the engine won't run. The electrical system is the weakest link of the three. More problems result from electrical breakdowns than from any other source. Keep that in mind before you begin tampering with carburetor adjustments and the like.

If a bike has been sitting for any length of time and refuses to start, check the battery (if the machine is so equipped) for a charged condition first, and then look to the gasoline delivery system. This includes the tank, fuel petcocks, lines, and the carburetor. Rust may have formed in the tank, obstructing fuel flow. Gasoline deposits may have gummed up carburetor jets and air passages. Gasoline tends to lose its potency after standing for long periods. Condensation may contaminate it with water. Drain old gas and try starting with a fresh tankful.

Compression, or the lack of it, usually enters the picture only in the case of older machines. Worn or broken pistons, rings, and cylinder bores could prevent starting. Generally a gradual power loss and harder and harder starting will be readily apparent in this case.

STARTING DIFFICULTIES

Check gas flow first. Remove the gas cap and look into the tank. If gas is present, pull off a fuel line at the carburetor and see if gas flows freely. If none comes out, the fuel tap may be shut off, blocked by rust or foreign matter, or the fuel line may be stopped up or kinked. If the carburetor is getting usable fuel, turn to the electrical system next.

Check that the battery is charged by turning on the lights or by beeping the horn. Refer to your owner's manual for starting procedures with a dead battery. Have the battery recharged if necessary.

Pull off the spark plug cap, remove the spark plug, and reconnect the cap. Lay the plug against the cylinder head so its base makes a good connection, and turn the engine over with the kickstarter. A fat, blue spark should jump across the electrodes. If there is no spark, or a weak one, there is electrical system trouble. Check for a defective plug by replacing it with a known good one. Don't assume a plug is good just because it's new.

Once the plug has been cleared of guilt, but there's still no spark, start backtracking through the system. If the contact at the end of the spark plug wire can be exposed, it can be held about ⅛ inch from the head while the engine is turned over to check for a spark. Remember to hold the wire only by its insulation to avoid a nasty shock. If the plug wires are dirty, greasy, or wet, wrap a rag around them so you don't get shocked. If you do feel a shock or see sparks along the wire, clean or replace the wire and/or its connections.

If there's no spark at the plug wire, look for loose connections at the coil and battery. If all

seems in order here, check next for oily or dirty contact points. Clean points with electrical contact cleaner, or a strip of paper. On battery ignition models, with the ignition switch turned on, open and close the points manually with a screwdriver.

No spark at the points with this test indicates a failure in the ignition system. Refer to Chapter Five (*Electrical System*) for checkout procedures for the entire system and individual components. Refer to the same chapter for checking and setting ignition timing.

Note that spark plugs of the incorrect heat range (too cold) may cause hard starting. Set gap to specifications. If you have just ridden through a puddle or washed the bike and it won't start, dry off the plug and plug wire. Water may have entered the carburetor and fouled the fuel under these conditions, but a wet plug and wire are the more likely problem.

If a healthy spark occurs at the right time, and there is adequate gas flow to the carburetor, check the carburetor itself at this time. Make sure all jets and air passages are clean, check float level, and adjust if necessary. Shake the float to check for gasoline inside it, and replace or repair as indicated. Check that the carburetor is mounted snugly, and no air is leaking past the mounting flange. Check for a clogged air filter.

Compression may be checked in the field by turning the kickstarter by hand and noting that an adequate resistance is felt, or by removing the spark plug and placing a finger over the plug hole and feeling for pressure.

An accurate compression check gives a good idea of the condition of the basic working parts of the engine. To perform this test, you need a compression gauge. The motor should be warm.

1. Remove the plug from the cylinder to be tested and clean out any dirt or grease.

2. Insert the tip of the gauge into the hole, making sure it is seated correctly.

3. Open the throttle all the way.

4. Crank the engine several times and record the highest pressure reading on the gauge. Refer to Chapter Two (*Periodic Maintenance*) to interpret results.

POOR IDLING

Poor idling may be caused by incorrect carburetor adjustment, incorrect timing, or ignition system defects. Check the gas cap vent for an obstruction. Also check for loose carburetor mounting bolts or a poor carburetor flange gasket.

MISFIRING

Misfiring can be caused by a weak spark or dirty plugs. Check for fuel contamination. Run the machine at night or in a darkened garage to check for spark leaks along the plug wires and under the spark plug cap. If misfiring occurs only at certain throttle settings, refer to the carburetor chapter for the specific carburetor circuits involved. Misfiring under heavy load, as when climbing hills or accelerating, is usually caused by bad spark plugs.

FLAT SPOTS

If the engine seems to die momentarily when the throttle is opened and then recovers, check for a dirty main jet in the carburetor, water in the fuel, or an excessively lean mixture.

POWER LOSS

Poor condition of rings, pistons, or cylinders will cause a lack of power and speed. Ignition timing should be checked.

OVERHEATING

If the engine seems to run too hot all the time, be sure you are not idling it for long periods. Air-cooled engines are not designed to operate at a standstill for any length of time. Heavy stop and go traffic is hard on a motorcycle engine. Spark plugs of the wrong heat range can burn pistons. An excessively lean gas mixture may cause overheating. Check ignition timing. Don't ride in too high a gear. Broken or worn rings may permit compression gases to leak past them, heating heads and cylinders excessively. Check oil level and use the proper grade lubricants.

BACKFIRING

Check that the timing is not advanced too far. Check fuel for contamination.

ENGINE NOISES

Experience is needed to diagnose accurately in this area. Noises are hard to differentiate and harder yet to describe. Deep knocking noises usually mean main bearing failure. A slapping noise generally comes from loose pistons. A light knocking noise during acceleration may be a bad connecting rod bearing. Pinging, which sounds like marbles being shaken in a tin can, is caused by ignition advanced too far or gasoline with too low an octane rating. Pinging should be corrected immediately or damage to pistons will result. Compression leaks at the head/cylinder joint will sound like a rapid on and off squeal.

PISTON SEIZURE

Piston seizure is caused by incorrect piston clearances when fitted, fitting rings with improper end gap, too thin an oil being used, incorrect spark plug heat range, or incorrect ignition timing. Overheating from any cause may result in seizure.

EXCESSIVE VIBRATION

Excessive vibration may be caused by loose motor mounts, worn engine or transmission bearings, loose wheels, worn swinging arm bushings, a generally poor running engine, broken or cracked frame, or one that has been damaged in a collision. See also *Poor Handling*.

CLUTCH SLIP OR DRAG

Clutch slip may be due to worn plates, improper adjustment, or glazed plates. A dragging clutch could result from damaged or bent plates, improper adjustment, or even clutch spring pressure.

POOR HANDLING

Poor handling may be caused by improper tire pressures, a damaged frame or swinging arm, worn shocks or front forks, weak fork springs, a bent or broken steering stem, misaligned wheels, loose or missing spokes, worn tires, bent handlebars, worn wheel bearings, or dragging brakes.

BRAKE PROBLEMS

Sticking brakes may be caused by broken or weak return springs, improper cable or rod adjustment, or dry pivot and cam bushings. Grabbing brakes may be caused by greasy linings which must be replaced. Brake grab may also be due to out-of-round drums or linings which have broken loose from the brake shoes. Glazed linings will cause loss of stopping power.

LIGHTING PROBLEMS

Bulbs which continuously burn out may be caused by excessive vibration, loose connections that permit sudden current surges, poor battery connections, or installation of the wrong type bulb.

A dead battery or one which discharges quickly may be caused by a faulty generator or rectifier. Check for loose or corroded terminals. Shorted battery cells or broken terminals will keep a battery from charging. Low water level will decrease a battery's capacity. A battery left uncharged after installation will sulphate, rendering it useless.

A majority of light and horn or other electrical accessory problems are caused by loose or corroded ground connections. Check those first, and then substitute known good units for easier troubleshooting.

TROUBLESHOOTING GUIDE

The following quick reference guide (**Table 1**) summarizes part of the troubleshooting process. Use this table to outline possible problem areas, then refer to the specific chapter or section involved.

7

Table 1   TROUBLESHOOTING GUIDE

Item	Problem or Cause	Things to Check
Loss of power	Poor compression	Piston rings and cylinder Head gaskets Crankcase leaks
	Overheated engine	Lubricating oil supply Clogged cooling fins Ignition timing Slipping clutch Carbon in combustion chamber
	Improper mixture	Dirty air cleaner Restricted fuel flow Gas cap vent hole
	Miscellaneous	Dragging brakes Tight wheel bearings Defective chain Clogged exhaust system
Steering	Hard steering	Tire pressures Steering damper adjustment Steering stem head Steering head bearings
		(continued)

Table 1   TROUBLESHOOTING GUIDE   (continued)

Item	Problem or Cause	Things to Check
Steering (continued)	Pulls to one side	Unbalanced shock absorbers Drive chain adjustment Front/rear wheel alignment Unbalanced tires Defective swing arm Defective steering head
	Shimmy	Drive chain adjustment Loose or missing spokes Deformed rims Worn wheel bearings Wheel balance
Gearshifting difficulties	Clutch	Adjustment Springs Friction plates Steel plates Oil quantity
	Transmission	Oil quantity Oil grade Return spring or pin Change lever or spring Drum position plate Change drum Change forks
Brakes	Poor brakes	Worn linings Brake adjustment Oil or water on brake linings Loose linkage or cables
	Noisy brakes	Worn or scratched lining Scratched brake drums Dirt in brakes
	Unadjustable brakes	Worn linings Worn drums Worn brake cams

A P P E N D I X

SPECIFICATIONS

This chapter contains specifications and performance figures for the various Yamaha models covered by this book. The tables are arranged in order of increasing engine size. Since there are differences between the various models, be sure to consult the correct table for the motorcycle in question.

SPECIFICATIONS — MODELS GT1 AND GT80A

DIMENSIONS

Overall length	63.4" (1,610mm)
Overall width	27.2" (690mm)
Overall height	36.6" (930mm)
Wheelbase	41.1" (1,045mm)
Road clearance	7.7" (195mm)

WEIGHT   141 lb.

PERFORMANCE

Maximum output	4.9 bhp @ 6,500 rpm
Maximum torque	4.0 ft.-lb. @ 6,000 rpm
Maximum speed	47 mph
Fuel consumption	176 mpg @ 19 mph

ENGINE

Type	7-port reed valve
Displacement	4.39 cu. in. (72cc)
Bore x stroke	1.850 x 1.654" (47 x 42mm)
Compression ratio	6.8 : 1

FUEL SYSTEM

Carburetor

Manufacturer, model	Teikei Y16P-3
Main jet	88 (GT80A=94)
Needle jet	2.080
Jet needle/clip position	049-2
Cutaway	1.0
Pilot jet	34
Air screw (no. of turns out)	1¾ (GT80A=1½)
Float level	21mm
Fuel tank capacity	1.3 U.S. gal., regular

LUBRICATION

Engine	Autolube
Transmission	500cc
Oil tank capacity	.7 qt.

IGNITION SYSTEM

Ignition type	Point-type magneto
Ignition timing	1.8mm
Spark plug type/gap	NGK B7HS/.020-.023" (.5-.6mm)

ELECTRICAL EQUIPMENT

Battery	6N4-2A (6V, 2 amp-hour)
Headlight	6V, 15W/15W
Tail/brake lamp	6V, 5.3W/6V, 25W
Turn signal lamp	6V, 17W
Neutral indicator lamp	6V, 3.0W
Speedometer lamp	6V, 3.0W
High beam indicator lamp	6V, 1.5W

TRANSMISSION SYSTEM

Primary reduction ratio	68/19 (3.578)

Transmission gear /overall ratios

1st gear	39/12 (34.064)
2nd gear	34/17 (20.962)
3rd gear	30/21 (14.973)
4th gear	27/24 (11.791)
Secondary reduction ratio	41/14 (2.928)

STEERING

Caster	63°
Trail	2.7" (68mm)

TIRES

Front	2.50 - 15, 4PR
Rear	2.75 - 14, 4PR

SPECIFICATIONS — MODELS GTMX AND GTMXA

DIMENSIONS			LUBRICATION	
Overall length	61.0″ (1,550mm)		Engine	Autolube
Overall width	27.2″ (690mm)		Transmission	500cc 10W/30 Type "SE"
Overall height	36.6″ (930mm)		Oil tank capacity	.7 qt.
Wheelbase	41.1″ (1,045mm)			
Road clearance	7.7″ (195mm)			

WEIGHT	132 lb.		IGNITION SYSTEM	
			Ignition type	Point-type magneto
			Ignition timing	1.8mm
PERFORMANCE			Spark plug type/gap	NGK B7HS/.020-.023″
Maximum output	4.9 bhp @ 6,500 rpm			(.5-.6mm)
Maximum torque	4.0 ft.-lb. @ 6,000 rpm			
Maximum speed	——			
Fuel consumption	——			

TRANSMISSION SYSTEM	
Primary reduction ratio	68/19 (3.758)

ENGINE		Transmission gear/overall ratios	
Type	7-port reed valve	1st gear	39/12 (34.064)
Displacement	4.39 cu. in. (72cc)	2nd gear	34/17 (20.962)
Bore x stroke	1.850 x 1.654″ (47 x 42mm)	3rd gear	30/21 (14.973)
Compression ratio	6.8 : 1	4th gear	27/24 (11.791)
		5th gear	N/A
		6th gear	N/A
		Secondary reduction ratio	41/14 (2.928)

FUEL SYSTEM				
Carburetor				
Manufacturer, model	Teikei Y16P-3			
Main jet	94 (GTMX before engine #2793=88)		STEERING	
Needle jet	2.080 (GTMX=2.085)		Caster	63°
Jet needle/clip position	049-2 (GTMX before engine #2793=029-1)		Trail	2.7″ (68mm)
Cutaway	1.0			
Pilot jet	34			
Air screw (no. of turns out)	1½ (GTMX before engine #2793=1¾)		TIRES	
Float level	21mm		Front	2.50 - 15, 4PR
Fuel tank capacity	1.3 U.S. gal., low lead		Rear	2.75 - 14, 4PR

8

SPECIFICATIONS — MODEL YZ80A

DIMENSIONS	
Overall length	66.9 in. (1,700mm)
Overall width	30.9 in. (785mm)
Overall height	36.8 in. (935mm)
Wheelbase	45.9 in. (1,165mm)
Ground clearance	6.3 in. (160mm)
WEIGHT	135 lb. (61 kg)
ENGINE	
Type	Air cooled, 2-stroke
Displacement	4.39 cu. in. (72cc)
Bore and stroke	1.850 x 1.654 in. (47 x 42mm)
TRANSMISSION	
Primary reduction	Gear, reduction ratio
	68/19 = (3.579)
Secondary reduction	Chain, reduction ratio
	43/14 = (3.071)
Gear ratios	
First	39/12 (3.250)
Second	34/17 (2.000)
Third	30/21 (1.429)
Fourth	27/24 (1.125)
Fifth	25/26 (0.961)
CHASSIS	
Suspension (front)	Telescopic
Suspension (rear)	Swing arm
Caster	61 degrees
Trail	3.4 in. (87mm)
Tire size, front	2.75 - 16
Tire size, rear	3.00 - 14
Gasoline tank capacity	1.1 gal. (4.3 liters)
Oil tank capacity	0.3 qt. (0.25 liter)

SPECIFICATIONS — MODEL YZ100C

DIMENSIONS	
Overall length	80.5 in.
Overall width	38.7 in.
Overall height	44.7 in.
Wheelbase	53.9 in.
Road clearance	10.8 in.
WEIGHT	190 lb.
ENGINE	
Bore x stroke	1.969 x 1.969 in.
Displacement	98cc
Compression ratio	7.2 to 1
FUEL SYSTEM	
Carburetor	VM30SS
Main jet	190
Needle jet	Q-2 (169)
Jet needle	6DP10-3
Pilot jet	40
Float level	0.59 in. (15mm)
IGNITION SYSTEM	
Type	CDI magneto
Timing	0.080 in. BTDC (2.0 ±0.15mm BTDC)
Spark plug	N59G
TRANSMISSION	
Primary reduction ratio	3.894 to 1
Gear ratios	
1st	2.538 to 1
2nd	1.933 to 1
3rd	1.555 to 1
4th	1.300 to 1
5th	1.142 to 1
6th	1.045 to 1
STEERING	
Caster	60 degrees
Trail	4.92 in.
TIRES	
Front	2.75-21
Rear	3.50-18

8

SPECIFICATIONS — DT100A

DIMENSIONS
Overall length	77.8″ (1,975mm)
Overall width	34.3″ (870mm)
Overall height	42.5″ (1,080mm)
Wheelbase	50.4″ (1,280mm)
Road clearance	8.9″ (225mm)

WEIGHT   201 lb.

PERFORMANCE
Maximum torque	7.0 ft.-lb. @ 7,000 rpm
Maximum speed	58 mph plus
Fuel consumption	153 mpg @ 31 mph

ENGINE
Type	7-port reed valve
Displacement	5.92 cu. in. (97cc)
Bore x stroke	2.047 x 1.795″ (52 x 45.6mm)
Compression ratio	6.8 : 1

FUEL SYSTEM

Carburetor
Manufacturer, model	Mikuni VM22SS
Main jet	150
Needle jet	N-4
Jet needle/clip position	4L6-2
Cutaway	1.5
Pilot jet	25
Air screw (no. of turns out)	1¼
Float level	20mm
Fuel tank capacity	1.6 U.S. gal., low lead

LUBRICATION
Engine	Autolube
Transmission	650cc
Oil tank capacity	1.3 qt.

IGNITION SYSTEM
Ignition type	Point-type magneto
Ignition timing	1.8mm
Spark plug type/gap	NGK B8HS/.020-.023″ (.5-.6mm)

ELECTRICAL EQUIPMENT
Battery	6N4B-2A (2 amp-hour)
Headlight	6V, 25W/25W
Tail/brake lamp	6V, 5.3W/6V, 17W
Turn signal lamp	6V, 17W
Neutral indicator lamp	6V, 3W
Speedometer lamp	6V, 3W
High beam indicator lamp	6V, 1.5W

TRANSMISSION SYSTEM
Primary reduction ratio	74/19 (3.894)
Transmission /overall ratios	
1st gear	35/11 (43.4)
2nd gear	30/15 (31.8)
3rd gear	26/19 (18.6)
4th gear	23/23 (13.6)
5th gear	20/25 (10.9)
6th gear	N/A
Secondary reduction ratio	49/14 (3.500)

STEERING
Caster	59°
Trail	5.2″ (132mm)

TIRES
Front	2.75 - 19, 4PR
Rear	3.00 - 18, 4PR

SPECIFICATIONS — MODEL MX100A

DIMENSIONS

Overall length	74.0" (1,880mm)
Overall width	34.1" (865mm)
Overall height	42.5" (1,080mm)
Wheelbase	49.6" (1,260mm)
Road clearance	8.3" (210mm)

WEIGHT   185 lbs.

PERFORMANCE

Maximum speed	——
Fuel consumption	——

ENGINE

Type	7-port reed valve
Displacement	5.92 cu. in. (97cc)
Bore x stroke	2.047 x 1.795" (52 x 45.6mm)
Compression ratio	6.8 : 1

FUEL SYSTEM

Carburetor	
Manufacturer, model	Mikuni VM26SC
Main jet	150
Needle jet	0-4
Jet needle/clip position	5F3-3
Cutaway	1.0
Pilot jet	50
Air screw (no. of turns out)	1½
Float level	15.8mm
Fuel tank capacity	1.6 U.S. gal., premium

LUBRICATION

Engine	Autolube
Transmission	650cc 10W/30 Type "SE"
Oil tank capacity	1.3 qt.

IGNITION SYSTEM

Ignition type	Point-type magneto
Ignition timing	2.0mm
Spark plug type/gap	NGK 138EV/.016" (.4mm)

TRANSMISSION SYSTEM

Primary reduction ratio	74/19 (3.894)
Transmission/overall ratios	
1st gear	34/12 (40.978)
2nd gear	30/16 (27.124)
3rd gear	26/19 (19.795)
4th gear	24/22 (15.781)
5th gear	22/23 (13.837)
6th gear	N/A
Secondary reduction ratio	52/14 (3.714)

STEERING

Caster	60°
Trail	5.4" (137mm)

TIRES

Front	2.75 - 21, 4PR
Rear	3.50 - 18, 4PR

8

SPECIFICATIONS — MODELS AT1, AT1-B, AND AT1-C

DIMENSIONS

Overall length	77.2" (1,960mm)
Overall width	35.8" (910mm)
Overall height	42.9" (1,090mm)
Wheelbase	50.6" (1,285mm)
Road clearance	8.9" (225mm)

WEIGHT   221 lb.

PERFORMANCE

Maximum output	11.5 bhp @ 7,500 rpm
Maximum torque	8.5 ft.-lb. @ 6,000 rpm
Maximum speed	60 mph plus
Fuel consumption	141 mpg @ 25 mph

ENGINE

Type	5-port piston/port induction
Displacement	7.51 cu. in. (123cc)
Bore x stroke	2.205 x 1.969" (56 x 50mm)
Compression ratio	7.1 : 1

FUEL SYSTEM

Carburetor

Manufacturer, model	Mikuni VM24SH
Main jet	150
Needle jet	N-8
Jet needle/clip position	4D3-3
Cutaway	2.0
Pilot jet	30
Air screw (no. of turns out)	1½
Float level	25.5mm
Fuel tank capacity	1.9 U.S. gal., low lead

LUBRICATION

Engine	Autolube
Transmission	750cc
Oil tank capacity	1.3 qt.

IGNITION SYSTEM

Ignition type	Battery/generator
Ignition timing	1.8mm fully advanced
Spark plug type/gap	NGK B8E/.020-.023" (.5-.6mm)

ELECTRICAL EQUIPMENT

Battery	6N4A-4D (12V, 4 amp-hour)
Headlight	6V, 25W/25W
Tail/brake lamp	6V, 5.3W/6V, 17W
Turn signal lamp	6V, 17W
Neutral indicator lamp	6V, 1.5W
Speedometer lamp	6V, 3W
High beam indicator lamp	6V, 1.5W

TRANSMISSION SYSTEM

Primary reduction ratio	74/19 (3.894)
Transmission gear/overall ratios	
1st gear	35/11 (39.81)
2nd gear	30/15 (25.03)
3rd gear	26/19 (17.12)
4th gear	23/23 (12.52)
5th gear	20/25 (10.01)
6th gear	N/A
Secondary reduction ratio	45/14 (3.214)

STEERING

Caster	60°
Trail	4.72" (120mm)

TIRES

Front	3.00 - 18, 4PR
Rear	3.25 - 18, 4PR

SPECIFICATIONS — MODELS AT1B-MX AND AT1C-MX

DIMENSIONS

Overall length	76.4″ (1,941mm)
Overall width	35.8″ (910mm)
Overall height	43.1″ (1,905mm)
Wheelbase	50.8″ (1,290mm)
Road clearance	9.1″ (231mm)

WEIGHT   202 lb.

PERFORMANCE

Maximum output	18 bhp @ 8,500 rpm
Maximum torque	11.4 ft.-lb. @ 7,500 rpm
Maximum speed	70 mph plus
Fuel consumption	——

ENGINE

Type	5-port piston/port induction
Displacement	7.51 cu. in. (123cc)
Bore x stroke	2.205 x 1.969″ (56 x 50mm)
Compression ratio	8.0 : 1

FUEL SYSTEM

Carburetor	
Manufacturer, model	Mikuni VM26SH
Main jet	190
Needle jet	0-5 (AT1C-MX=0-2)
Jet needle/clip position	4F15-3 (AT1C-MX=4F15-2)
Cutaway	1.5
Pilot jet	30
Air screw (no. of turns out)	1½
Float level	25.5mm
Fuel tank capacity	1.9 U.S. gal., premium

LUBRICATION

Engine	Autolube
Transmission	750cc 10W/30 Type "SE"
Oil tank capacity	1.3 qt.

IGNITION SYSTEM

Ignition type	Point-type magneto
Ignition timing	2.0mm
Spark plug type/gap	NGK B9EN/.020-.023″ (.5-.6mm)

TRANSMISSION SYSTEM

Primary reduction ratio	74/19 (3.894)
Transmission gear/overall ratios	
1st gear	34/12 (33.10)
2nd gear	30/16 (21.90)
3rd gear	26/19 (15.98)
4th gear	24/22 (12.76)
5th gear	22/23 (11.18)
6th gear	N/A
Secondary reduction ratios	45/15 (3.000)

STEERING

Caster	60°
Trail	4.84″ (123mm)

TIRES

Front	3.25 - 18, 4PR
Rear	3.50 - 18, 4PR

8

SPECIFICATIONS — MODEL AT1M

DIMENSIONS

Overall length	76.4″ (1,941mm)
Overall width	35.8″ (909mm)
Overall height	43.1″ (1,095mm)
Wheelbase	50.8″ (1,290mm)
Road clearance	9.1″ (231mm)

WEIGHT   202 lb.

PERFORMANCE

Maximum output	18 bhp @ 8,500 rpm
Maximum torque	11.4 ft.-lb. @ 7,500 rpm
Maximum speed	70 mph plus
Fuel consumption	——

ENGINE

Type	5-port piston/port induction
Displacement	7.51 cu. in. (123cc)
Bore x stroke	2.205 x 1.969″ (56 x 50mm)
Compression ratio	7.1 : 1

FUEL SYSTEM

Carburetor

Manufacturer, model	Mikuni VM26SH
Main jet	170
Needle jet	0-2
Jet needle/clip position	4D3-3
Cutaway	1.5
Pilot jet	30
Air screw (no. of turns out)	1½
Float level	25.5mm
Fuel tank capacity	1.9 U.S. gal., low lead

LUBRICATION

Engine	Autolube
Transmission	750cc
Oil tank capacity	1.3 qt.

IGNITION SYSTEM

Ignition type	Point-type magneto
Ignition timing	2.0mm
Spark plug type/gap	NGK B9E/.020-.023″ (.5-.6mm)

TRANSMISSION SYSTEM

Primary reduction ratio	74/19 (3.894)

Transmission gear/overall ratios

1st gear	35/11 (33.10)
2nd gear	30/15 (21.91)
3rd gear	26/19 (15.99)
4th gear	23/23 (12.76)
5th gear	20/25 (11.18)
6th gear	N/A
Secondary reduction ratio	45/15 (3.000)

STEERING

Caster	60°
Trail	4.84″ (123mm)

TIRES

Front	3.25 - 18, 4PR
Rear	3.50 - 18, 4PR

SPECIFICATIONS — MODELS AT2 AND AT3

DIMENSIONS

Overall length	77.2″ (1,960mm)
Overall width	35.8″ (910mm)
Overall height	42.9″ (1,090mm)
Wheelbase	50.6″ (1,285mm)
Road clearance	8.9″ (225mm)

WEIGHT

221 lb.

PERFORMANCE

Maximum output	13 bhp @ 7,000 rpm
Maximum torque	10 ft.-lb. @ 6,000 rpm
Maximum speed	65 mph plus
Fuel consumption	129 mpg @ 31 mph

ENGINE

Type	7-port reed valve
Displacement	7.51 cu. in. (123cc)
Bore x stroke	2.205 x 1.969″ (56 x 50mm)
Compression ratio	7.1 : 1

FUEL SYSTEM

Carburetor	
Manufacturer, model	Mikuni VM26SH
Main jet	230
Needle jet	0-6
Jet needle/clip position	5J3-3
Cutaway	1.5
Pilot jet	25
Air screw (no. of turns out)	1¾
Float level	21mm
Fuel tank capacity	1.9 U.S. gal., low lead

LUBRICATION

Engine	Autolube
Transmission	600cc
Oil tank capacity	1.3 qt.

IGNITION SYSTEM

Ignition type	Battery/generator
Ignition timing	1.8mm
Spark plug type/gap	NGK B8ES/.020-.023″ (.5-.6mm)

ELECTRICAL EQUIPMENT

Battery	12N7-3B (12V, 7 amp-hour)
Headlight	12V, 25W/25W
Tail/brake lamp	12V, 7W/12V, 27W
Turn signal lamp	12V, 27W
Neutral indicator lamp	12V, 3W
Speedometer lamp	12V, 3W
High beam indicator lamp	12V, 2W

TRANSMISSION SYSTEM

Primary reduction ratio	74/19 (3.894)
Transmission gear/overall ratios	
1st gear	35/11 (39.824)
2nd gear	30/15 (25.031)
3rd gear	26/19 (17.121)
4th gear	23/23 (12.515)
5th gear	20/25 (10.012)
6th gear	N/A
Secondary reduction ratio	45/15 (3.000)

STEERING

Caster	60°
Trail	4.7″

TIRES

Front	3.00 - 18, 4PR
Rear	3.25 - 18, 4PR

8

SPECIFICATIONS — MODEL AT2-MX

DIMENSIONS

Overall length	76.4" (1,941mm)
Overall width	35.8" (910mm)
Overall height	43.1" (1,905mm)
Wheelbase	50.8" (1,290mm)
Road clearance	9.1" (231mm)

WEIGHT	202 lb.

PERFORMANCE

Maximum output	20 bhp @ 8,500 rpm
Maximum torque	12.3 ft-lb. @ 8,000 rpm
Maximum speed	——
Fuel consumption	——

ENGINE

Type	7-port reed valve
Displacement	7.51 cu. in. (123cc)
Bore x stroke	2.205 x 1.969" (56 x 50mm)
Compression ratio	7.8 : 1

FUEL SYSTEM

Carburetor

Manufacturer, model	Mikuni VM26SC
Main jet	190
Needle jet	N-8
Jet needle/clip position	4F15-3
Cutaway	2.5
Pilot jet	60
Air screw (no. of turns out)	1.0
Float level	15.1mm
Fuel tank capacity	1.8 U.S. gal., premium

LUBRICATION

Engine	Autolube
Transmission	750cc 10W/30 type "SE"
Oil tank capacity	1.3 qt.

IGNITION SYSTEM

Ignition type	Point-type magneto
Ignition timing	2.0mm
Spark plug type/gap	NGK B9EN/.020-.023" (.5-.6mm)

TRANSMISSION SYSTEM

Primary reduction ratio	74/19 (3.894)
Transmission gear/overall ratios	
1st gear	34/12 (35.456)
2nd gear	30/16 (23.446)
3rd gear	26/19 (17.121)
4th gear	24/22 (13.654)
5th gear	22/23 (11.964)
6th gear	N/A
Secondary reduction ratio	45/14 (3.214)

STEERING

Caster	60°
Trail	4.84" (123mm)

TIRES

Front	2.75 - 21, 4PR
Rear	3.50 - 18, 4PR

SPECIFICATIONS — MODEL ATMX

DIMENSIONS

Overall length	74.4" (1,965mm)
Overall width	35.8" (910mm)
Overall height	44.1" (1,120mm)
Wheelbase	50.8" (1,290mm)
Road clearance	9.4" (240mm)

WEIGHT   203 lb.

PERFORMANCE

Maximum output	20 bhp @ 8,500 rpm
Maximum torque	12.3 ft.-lb. @ 8,000 rpm
Maximum speed	——
Fuel consumption	——

ENGINE

Type	7-port reed valve
Displacement	7.51 cu. in. (123cc)
Bore x stroke	2.205 x 1.969" (56 x 50mm)
Compression ratio	7.8 : 1

FUEL SYSTEM

Carburetor

Manufacturer, model	Mikuni VM26SC
Main jet	190
Needle jet	N-8
Jet needle/clip position	4F15-3
Cutaway	2.5
Pilot jet	60
Air screw (no. of turns out)	1.0
Float level	25mm
Fuel tank capacity	1.8 U.S. gal., premium

LUBRICATION

Engine	Autolube
Transmission	750cc 10W/30 type "SE"
Oil tank capacity	1.3 qt.

IGNITION SYSTEM

Ignition type	Point-type magneto
Ignition timing	2.0mm
Spark plug type/gap	NGK B9EN/.020-.023" (.5-.6mm)

TRANSMISSION SYSTEM

Primary reduction ratio	74/19 (3.894)

Transmission gear/overall ratios

1st gear	34/12 (35.456)
2nd gear	30/16 (23.446)
3rd gear	26/19 (17.121)
4th gear	24/22 (13.654)
5th gear	22/23 (11.964)
6th gear	N/A
Secondary reduction ratio	45/14 (3.214)

STEERING

Caster	60°
Trail	5.4"

TIRES

Front	2.75 - 21, 4PR
Rear	3.50 - 18, 4PR

8

SPECIFICATIONS — MODEL DT125A

DIMENSIONS

Overall length	79.3" (2,015mm)
Overall width	34.3" (870mm)
Overall height	42.5" (1,080mm)
Wheelbase	51.6" (1,310mm)
Road clearance	9.1" (230mm)

WEIGHT   227 lb.

PERFORMANCE

Fuel consumption	129 mpg @ 31 mph

ENGINE

Type	7-port reed valve
Displacement	7.51 cu. in. (123cc)
Bore x stroke	2.205 x 1.969" (56 x 50mm)
Compression ratio	7.1 : 1

FUEL SYSTEM

Carburetor

Manufacturer, model	Mikuni VM24SH
Main jet	140
Needle jet	0-0
Jet needle/clip position	4G2-3
Cutaway	2.0
Pilot jet	2.5
Air screw (no. of turns out)	1½
Float level	20mm
Fuel tank capacity	1.8 U.S. gal., low lead

LUBRICATION

Engine	Autolube
Transmission	750cc
Oil tank capacity	1.3 qt.

IGNITION SYSTEM

Ignition type	Battery/generator
Ignition timing	1.8mm, fully advanced
Spark plug type/gap	NGK B8ES/.020-.023" (.5-.6mm)

ELECTRICAL EQUIPMENT

Battery	12N7-3B (12V, 7 amp-hour)
Headlight	12V, 25W/25W
Tail/brake lamp	12V, 8.3W/12V, 27W
Turn signal lamp	12V, 27W
Neutral indicator lamp	12V, 3W
Speedometer lamp	12V, 3W
High beam indicator lamp	12V, 3W

TRANSMISSION SYSTEM

Primary reduction ratio	74/19 (3.894)
Transmission gear/overall ratios	
1st gear	35/11 (39.81)
2nd gear	30/15 (25.03)
3rd gear	26/19 (17.12)
4th gear	23/23 (12.52)
5th gear	20/25 (10.01)
6th gear	N/A
Secondary reduction ratio	45/14 (3.214)

STEERING

Caster	59°
Trail	4.88" (124mm)

TIRES

Front	3.00 - 19, 4PR
Rear	3.25 - 18, 4PR

SPECIFICATIONS — MODEL MX125A

DIMENSIONS

Overall length	74.4" (1,965mm)
Overall width	35.8" (910mm)
Overall height	44.1" (1,120mm)
Wheelbase	50.8" (1,290mm)
Road clearance	9.4" (240mm)

WEIGHT

	202 lb.

PERFORMANCE

Maximum speed	——
Fuel consumption	——

ENGINE

Type	7-port reed valve
Displacement	7.51 cu. in. (123cc)
Bore x stroke	2.205 x 1.969" (56 x 50mm)
Compression ratio	N/A

FUEL SYSTEM

Carburetor	
Manufacturer, model	Mikuni VM28SC
Main jet	180
Needle jet	N-8
Jet needle/clip position	5F3-3
Cutaway	2.5
Pilot jet	60
Float level	1.0
Fuel tank capacity	1.6 U.S. gal., premium

LUBRICATION

Engine	Autolube
Transmission	650cc 10W/30 Type "SE"
Oil tank capacity	1 pt. (450cc)

IGNITION SYSTEM

Ignition type	Point-type magneto
Ignition timing	2.0mm
Spark plug type/gap	NGK B9EV/.020-.023" (.5-.6mm)

TRANSMISSION SYSTEM

Primary reduction ratio	74/19 (3.894)
Transmission gear/overall ratios	
1st gear	34/12 (34.576)
2nd gear	30/16 (22.882)
3rd gear	26/19 (16.670)
4th gear	24/22 (13.313)
5th gear	22/23 (11.673)
6th gear	N/A
Secondary reduction ratio	47/15 (3.133)

STEERING

Caster	60°
Trail	5.4" (137mm)

TIRES

Front	2.75 - 21, 4PR
Rear	3.50 - 18, 4PR

8

SPECIFICATIONS — MODEL YZ125A

DIMENSIONS

Overall length	79.3″ (2,014mm)
Overall width	36.4″ (924mm)
Overall height	43.3″ (1,100mm)
Wheelbase	53.0″ (1,346mm)
Road clearance	10.2″ (259mm)

WEIGHT   176 lb.

PERFORMANCE

Maximum speed	——
Fuel consumption	——

ENGINE

Type	7-port reed valve
Displacement	7.51 cu. in. (123cc)
Bore x stroke	2.205 x 1.969″ (56 x 50mm)
Compression ratio	8.0 : 1

FUEL SYSTEM

Carburetor	
Manufacturer, model	Mikuni VM28SC
Main jet	190
Needle jet	N-8
Jet needle/clip position	5F3-3
Cutaway	2.5
Pilot jet	60
Air screw (no. of turns out)	1.0
Float level	.622″ (15.8mm)
Fuel tank capacity	1.45 U.S. gal.

LUBRICATION

Engine	15 : 1 pre-mix
Transmission	650cc 10W/30, Type "SE"
Oil tank capacity	N/A

IGNITION SYSTEM

Ignition type	CDI magneto
Ignition timing	2.0mm
Spark plug type/gap	B8EV

TRANSMISSION SYSTEM

Primary reduction ratio	74/19 (3.894)
Transmission gear/overall ratios	
1st gear	34/12 (2.833)
2nd gear	31/15 (2.066)
3rd gear	29/18 (1.611)
4th gear	25/19 (1.315)
5th gear	24/21 (1.142)
Secondary reduction ratio	47/14 (3.357)

STEERING

Caster	60°
Trail	5.51″

TIRES

Front	2.75 - 21, 4PR
Rear	3.50 - 18, 4PR

SPECIFICATIONS — CT1, CT1-B, AND CT1-C

DIMENSIONS

Overall length	77.4" (1,965mm)
Overall width	35.8" (910mm)
Overall height	43.1" (1,095mm)
Wheelbase	50.6" (1,285mm)
Road clearance	9.1" (230mm)

WEIGHT   211 lb.

PERFORMANCE

Maximum output	15.6 bhp @ 7,000 rpm
Maximum torque	11.9 ft.-lb. @ 5,500 rpm
Maximum speed	65 mph plus
Fuel consumption	129 mpg @ 25 mph

ENGINE

Type	5-port piston/port induction
Displacement	10.43 cu. in. (171cc)
Bore x stroke	2.598 x 1.969" (66 x 50mm)
Compression ratio	6.8 : 1

FUEL SYSTEM

Carburetor	
Manufacturer, model	Mikuni VM24SH
Main jet	150
Needle jet	N-8
Jet needle/clip position	4D3-3
Cutaway	2.0
Pilot jet	30
Air screw (no. of turns out)	1½
Float level	25.5mm
Fuel tank capacity	1.9 U.S. gal., low lead

LUBRICATION

Engine	Autolube
Transmission	750cc
Oil tank capacity	1.3 qt.

IGNITION SYSTEM

Ignition type	Point-type magneto
Ignition timing	1.8mm
Spark plug type/gap	NGK B8ES/.020-.023" (.5-.6mm)

ELECTRICAL EQUIPMENT

Battery	MVI-6D (6V, 2 amp-hour)
Headlight	6V, 25W/25W
Tail/brake lamp	6V, 7W/6V, 23W
Turn signal lamp	6V, 8W (CT1-C)
Speedometer lamp	6V, 1.5W
High beam indicator lamp	6V, 1.5W

TRANSMISSION SYSTEM

Primary reduction ratio	74/19 (3.894)
Transmission gear/overall ratios	
1st gear	35/11 (34.95)
2nd gear	30/15 (21.90)
3rd gear	26/19 (14.99)
4th gear	23/23 (10.93)
5th gear	20/23 (8.76)
6th gear	N/A
Secondary reduction ratio	45/16 (2.813)

STEERING

Caster	60°
Trail	4.8" (123mm)

TIRES

Front	3.25 - 18, 4PR
Rear	3.50 - 18, 4PR

8

SPECIFICATIONS — MODELS CT2 AND CT3

DIMENSIONS

Overall length	78.0″ (1,981mm)
Overall width	35.8″ (909mm)
Overall height	43.7″ (1,110mm)
Wheelbase	50.8″ (1,290mm)
Road clearance	9.4″ (239mm)

WEIGHT 214 lb.

PERFORMANCE

Maximum output	16 bhp @ 7,500 rpm
Maximum torque	11.9 ft.-lb. @ 6,000 rpm
Maximum speed	65 mph plus
Fuel consumption	129 mpg @ 31 mph

ENGINE

Type	7-port reed valve
Displacement	10.43 cu. in. (171cc)
Bore x stroke	2.508 x 1.969″
	(66 x 50mm)
Compression ratio	6.8 : 1

FUEL SYSTEM

Carburetor

Manufacturer, model	Mikuni VM24SH
Main jet	230
Needle jet	0-6
Jet needle/clip position	4J13-2
Cutaway	2.0
Pilot jet	25
Air screw (no. of turns out)	2.0
Float level	21mm
Fuel tank capacity	1.8 U.S. gal., low lead

LUBRICATION

Engine	Autolube
Transmission	600cc
Oil tank capacity	1.3 qt.

IGNITION SYSTEM

Ignition type	Point-type magneto
Ignition timing	1.8mm
Spark plug type/gap	NGK B8ES/.020-.023″
	(.5-.6mm)

ELECTRICAL EQUIPMENT

Battery	6N4A-40 (6V, 4 amp-hour)
Headlight	6V, 25W/25W
Tail/brake lamp	6V, 5W/6V, 5W
Turn signal lamp	6V, 8W
Neutral indicator lamp	6V, 15W
Speedometer lamp	6V, 3W
High beam indicator lamp	6V, 1.5W

TRANSMISSION SYSTEM

Primary reduction ratio	74/19 (3.894)

Transmission gear/overall ratios

1st gear	35/11 (34.865)
2nd gear	30/15 (21.914)
3rd gear	26/19 (14.989)
4th gear	23/23 (10.957)
5th gear	20/25 (8.766)
6th gear	N/A
Secondary reduction ratio	45/16 (2.812)

STEERING

Caster	60°
Trail	4.8″ (123mm)

TIRES

Front	3.25 - 18, 4PR
Rear	3.50 - 18, 4PR

SPECIFICATIONS — MODEL DT175A

DIMENSIONS

Overall length	79.5" (2,020mm)
Overall width	34.3" (870mm)
Overall height	42.9" (1,090mm)
Wheelbase	52.2" (1,330mm)
Road clearance	9.1" (230mm)

WEIGHT   214 lb.

PERFORMANCE

Fuel consumption	117 mpg @ 31 mph

ENGINE

Type	7-port reed valve
Displacement	10.43 cu. in. (171cc)
Bore x stroke	2.598 x 1.969" (66 x 50mm)
Compression ratio	6.8 : 1

FUEL SYSTEM

Carburetor

Manufacturer, model	Mikuni VM24SS
Main jet	160
Needle jet	O-2
Jet needle/clip position	5G4-3
Cutaway	2.0
Pilot jet	25
Air screw (no. of turns out)	1¾
Float level	20mm
Fuel tank capacity	1.8 U.S. gal., low lead

LUBRICATION

Engine	Autolube
Transmission	650cc
Oil tank capacity	1.3 qt.

IGNITION SYSTEM

Ignition type	Point-type magneto
Ignition timing	1.8mm
Spark plug type/gap	NGK B8ES/.020-.023" (.5-.6mm)

ELECTRICAL EQUIPMENT

Battery	6N4B-ZA (6V, 4 amp-hour)
Headlight	6V, 25W/25W
Tail/brake lamp	6V, 5.3W/6V, 17W
Turn signal lamp	6V, 17W
Neutral indicator lamp	6V, 1.5W
Speedometer lamp	6V, 3W
High beam indicator lamp	6V, 1.5W

TRANSMISSION SYSTEM

Primary reduction ratio	74/19 (3.894)

Transmission gear/overall ratios

1st gear	35/11
2nd gear	30/15
3rd gear	26/19
4th gear	23/23
5th gear	20/25
6th gear	N/A
Secondary reduction ratio	45/16 (2.812)

STEERING

Caster	59°
Trail	4.8" (122mm)

TIRES

Front	3.00 - 19, 4PR
Rear	3.50 - 18, 4PR

8

SPECIFICATIONS — MODEL MX175A

DIMENSIONS		IGNITION SYSTEM	
Overall length	79.3" (2,015mm)	Ignition type	CDI magneto
Overall width	36.4" (925mm)	Ignition timing	2.0mm
Overall height	43.3" (1,100mm)	Spark plug type/gap	NGK B8EV/.016" (.4mm)
Wheelbase	52.9" (1,345mm)		
Road clearance	9.4" (260mm)	FUEL SYSTEM	
		Carburetor	
WEIGHT	N/A	Manufacturer, model	VM28SC
		Main jet	180
PERFORMANCE		Needle jet	N-8
Maximum speed	——	Jet needle/clip position	5F3-3
Fuel consumption	N/A	Cutaway	2.5
		Pilot jet	60
		Air screw (no. of turns out)	1.0
		Float level	15.8mm
ENGINE		Fuel tank capacity	1.6 U.S. gal., premium
Type	7-port reed valve		
Displacement	10.33 cu. in. (171cc)	TRANSMISSION SYSTEM	
Bore x stroke	2.600 x 1.969" (66 x 50mm)	Primary reduction ratio	74/19 (3.894)
		Transmission gear/overall ratios	
FUEL SYSTEM		1st gear	34/12
Carburetor		2nd gear	31/15
Manufacturer, model	VM28SC	3rd gear	29/18
Main jet	180	4th gear	25/19
Needle jet	N-8	5th gear	24/21
Jet needle/clip position	5F3-3	6th gear	N/A
Cutaway	2.5	Secondary reduction ratio	47/14 (3.357)
Pilot jet	60		
Air screw (no. of turns out)	1.0	STEERING	
Float level	15.8mm	Caster	60°
Fuel tank capacity	1.6 U.S. gal., premium	Trail	5.5" (140mm)
LUBRICATION		TIRES	
Engine	Autolube	Front	2.75 - 21, 4PR
Transmission	650cc 10W/30 Type "SE"	Rear	3.50 - 21, 4PR
Oil tank capacity	1.3 qt.		

INDEX

A

Air cleaner 18-19
Autolube cable adjustment 21
Autolube pump 20
Autolube system 26-27

B

Backfiring 130
Battery 21, 101-104
Battery ignition timing 17
Brake lights 100-101
Brakes
    Adjustment 113
    Inspection 112
    Modification, rear brake 114
    Operation 112
    Shoes 112-113
    Troubleshooting 131
Breaker points 14

C

Capacitor discharge ignition 95
Carbon removal 12-14
Carburetor
    Component section 86-87
    Float level adjustment 84-85
    Independent float carburetor 79-81
    Operation 74-77
    Overhaul, general 77-79
    Problems 87
    Single-unit float carburetor 81-84
    Tune-up 19-20
CDI timing 17-18
Chassis
    Brakes 112-114
    Drive chain 126-127
    Forks, front 114-120
    Steering head 120
    Suspension, rear 120-126
    Wheels 105-112

Clutch
    Adjustment 21
    Description 37
    Disassembly 41-42
    Inspection 42-43
    Installation 44
    Slip or drag 130
Compression test 11
Connecting rod 150
Crankcase
    Assembly 60
    Inspection 59-60
    Separating halves 57-59
Crankcase cover, right 37
Crankshaft
    Alignment 71-73
    Inspection 68
    Overhaul 68-71
    Removal 67
    Runout 68
Cylinder and cylinder head 28-30

D

Drive chain 126-127

E

Electrical system
    Battery 101-104
    Capacitor discharge ignition 95
    Flywheel magneto operation 89-91
    Horn 101
    Lights 100-101
    Magneto troubleshooting 91-95
    Main switch 101
    Main switch 101
    Starter/generator 95-100
    Wiring diagrams .... 96, 99, 100, end of book

9

Engine
    Crankcase 57-60
    Crankcase cover, right 37
    Crankshaft 67-73
    Cylinder and cylinder head 28-30
    Disassembly, preparation for 27
    Flywheel magneto and starter/generator . 35-36
    Lubrication 25-27
    Noises, unusual 130
    Operating principles, 2-stroke engine 23-25
    Piston, pin and rings 30-34
    Reed valve 34-35
    Removal 27-28
    Sprocket 36

F

Flat spots 130
Flywheel magneto ignition system
    Charging circuit test 94-95
    Coil 94
    Condenser 94
    Disassembly 91-94
    Ignition timing 16
    Lighting and charging coil 94
    Magneto, removal and installation 35-36
    Operation 89-91
    Rectifier 95
Fork, front
    Disassembly 117
    Inspection 117-119
    Oil change 119-120
    Oil seal 119
    Reassembly 119
    Removal 114-116
Fuel and oil mixture 26
Fuel strainer 19

G

General information 1-7

H

Handling, poor 131
Headlight 100
Horn 101

I

Idling, poor 130
Ignition timing
    Battery ignition 17
    CDI 17-18
    Magneto ignition 16

K

Kickstarter 44-48

L

Lighting problems 131
Lights 100-101
Lubrication system, engine 25-27

M

Magneto (see Flywheel magneto ignition system)
Maintenance and tune-up
    Air cleaner service 18-19
    Autolube cable adjustment 21
    Autolube pump 20
    Battery ignition timing 17
    Battery service 21
    Brakes 22
    Breaker points 14-15
    Carbon removal 12-14
    Carburetor adjustment 19-20
    CDI timing 17-18
    Clutch adjustment 21
    Compression test 11
    Drive chain 21-22
    Electrical equipment 21
    Fuel strainer 19
    Magneto ignition timing 16
    Oil change 21
    Spark plug 8-11
    Throttle cable adjustment 20
Main switch 101
Misfiring 130

O

Oil change 21
Overheating 130

P

Piston, pin and rings
    Clearance 34
    Installation 34
    Pin 34
    Piston seizure 130
    Reconditioning 33
    Removal 30
    Rings 31-33
Power loss 130
Primary drive gear 44

R

Reed valve 34-35

S

Safety hints 2
Screws and fasteners 5-7
Service hints 1-2
Shifter 48-57
Shock absorbers, rear 120-126
Spark plugs 8-11
Specifications
  ATMX 145
  AT1, AT1-B, and AT1-C 140
  AT1B-MX and AT1C-MX 141
  AT1M 142
  AT2 and AT3 143
  AT2-MX 144
  CT1, CT1-B, and CT1-C 149
  CT2 and CT3 150
  DT100A 138
  DT125A 146
  DT175A 151
  GTMX and GTMXA 135
  GT1 and GT80A 134
  MX100A 139
  MX125A 147
  MX175A 152
  YZ80A 136
  YZ100C 137
  YZ125A 148
Spokes 107
Sprocket, engine 36
Starter/generator
  Armature 96-99
  Choke coil 100
  Description 95-96
  Generator output 96
  Removal and installation 36
  Starter troubleshooting 100
  Voltage regulator 99-100
  Yoke, checking 96
Starting difficulties 129
Steering head 120
Supplies, expendable 5
  Shock absorbers 120-126
  Swing arm 126

T

Tachometer drive gear 48
Throttle cable adjustment 20
Timing 16-18
Tools 2-5
Transmission
  Description 60-64
  End play adjustment 65-67
  Inspection and installation 65
  Removal 64-65
  Troubleshooting 67
Troubleshooting
  Backfiring 130
  Brake problems 131
  Clutch slip or drag
  Engine noises 130
  Excessive vibration 130
  Flat spots 130
  Lighting problems 131
  Misfiring 130
  Operating difficulties 130-131
  Operating requirements 128-129
  Overheating 130
  Piston seizure 130
  Poor handling 130
  Poor idling 130
  Power loss 130
  Starting difficulties 129
  Troubleshooting guide 131-132
Tune-up (see maintenance and tune-up)
Turn signals 100

W

Wheels
  Balance 110
  Bead protectors 107
  Bearings, front 111
  Checks 111
  Clutch hub bearings 111
  Hub cushions, rear 111-112
  Removal, front 105
  Removal, rear 107
  Rims 107-110
  Runout 110
  Spokes 107
  Sprocket, rear 112
Wiring diagrams .... 96, 99, 100, end of book

9

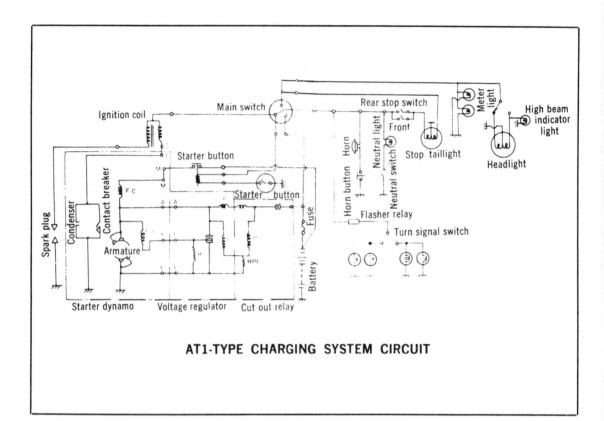

AT1-TYPE CHARGING SYSTEM CIRCUIT

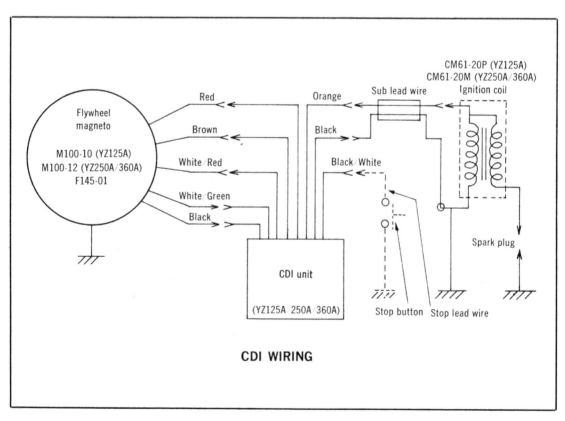

CDI WIRING

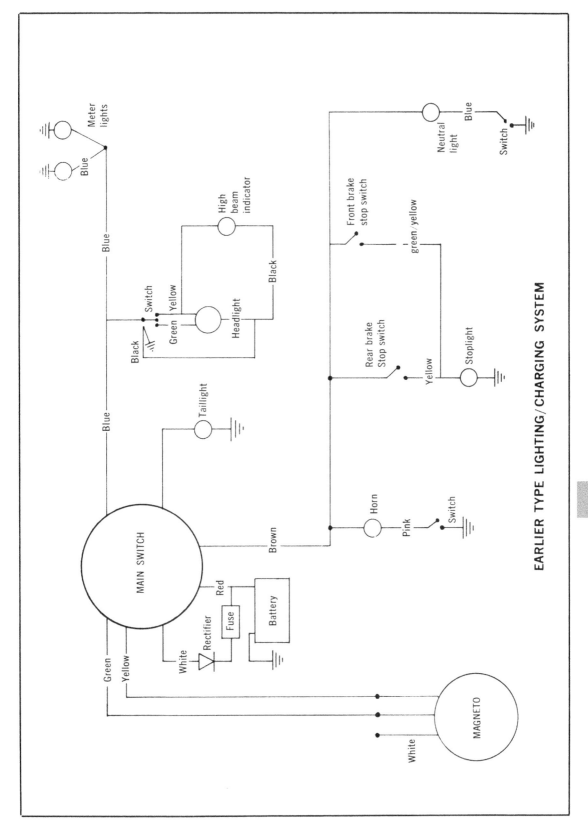

EARLIER TYPE LIGHTING/CHARGING SYSTEM

10

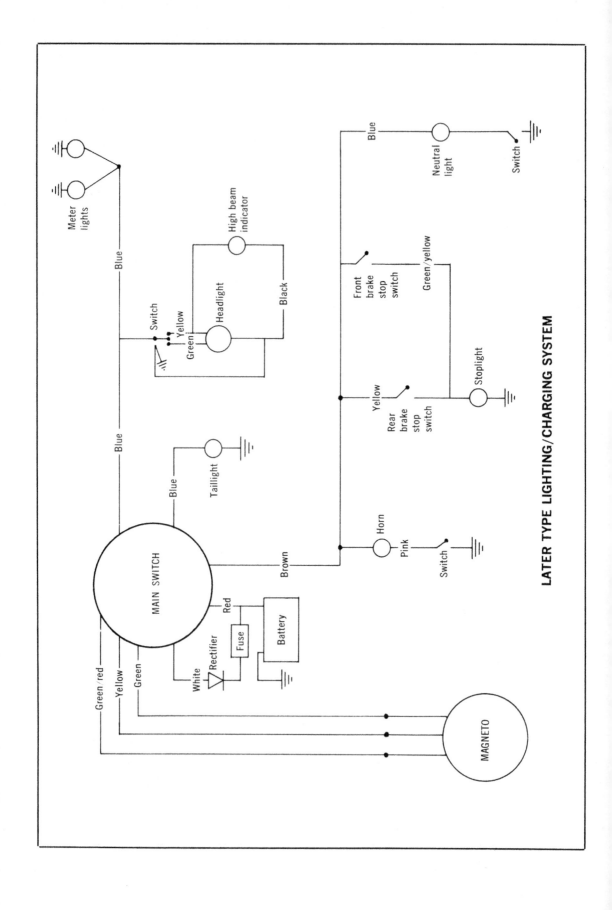

LATER TYPE LIGHTING/CHARGING SYSTEM

MAINTENANCE LOG

Date	Miles	Type of Service

BMW

M308	500 & 600cc Twins, 55-69
M502-3	BMW R50/5-R100GS PD, 70-96
M500-3	BMW K-Series, 85-97
M501-2	K1200RS, GT & LT, 98-08
M503-3	R850, R1100, R1150 & R1200C, 93-05
M309	F650, 1994-2000

HARLEY-DAVIDSON

M419	Sportsters, 59-85
M429-5	XL/XLH Sportster, 86-03
M427-2	XL Sportster, 04-09
M418	Panheads, 48-65
M420	Shovelheads,66-84
M421-3	FLS/FXS Evolution,84-99
M423-2	FLS/FXS Twin Cam, 00-05
M250	FLS/FXS/FXC Softail, 06-09
M422-3	FLH/FLT/FXR Evolution, 84-98
M430-4	FLH/FLT Twin Cam, 99-05
M426	VRSC Series, 02-07
M424-2	FXD Evolution, 91-98
M425-3	FXD Twin Cam, 99-05

HONDA

ATVs

M316	Odyssey FL250, 77-84
M311	ATC, TRX & Fourtrax 70-125, 70-87
M433	Fourtrax 90, 93-00
M326	ATC185 & 200, 80-86
M347	ATC200X & Fourtrax 200SX, 86-88
M455	ATC250 & Fourtrax 200/250, 84-87
M342	ATC250R, 81-84
M348	TRX250R/Fourtrax 250R & ATC250R, 85-89
M456-4	TRX250X 87-92; TRX300EX 93-06
M446-3	TRX250 Recon & Recon ES, 97-07
M215	TRX250EX, 01-05
M346-3	TRX300/Fourtrax 300 & TRX300FW/Fourtrax 4x4,88-00
M200-2	TRX350 Rancher, 00-06
M459-3	TRX400 Foreman 95-03
M454-4	TRX400EX 99-07
M205	TRX450 Foreman, 98-04
M210	TRX500 Rubicon, 01-04

Singles

M310-13	50-110cc OHC Singles, 65-99
M315	100-350cc OHC, 69-82
M317	125-250cc Elsinore, 73-80
M442	CR60-125R Pro-Link, 81-88
M431-2	CR80R, 89-95, CR125R, 89-91
M435	CR80R &CR80RB, 96-02
M457-2	CR125R, 92-97; CR250R, 92-96
M464	CR125R, 1998-2002
M443	CR250R-500R Pro-Link, 81-87
M432-3	CR250R, 88-91 & CR500R, 88-01
M437	CR250R, 97-01
M352	CRF250R, CRF250X, CRF450R & CRF450X, 02-05
M319-2	XR50R, CRF50F, XR70R & CRF70F, 97-05
M312-14	XL/XR75-100, 75-91
M222	XR80R, CRF80F, XR100R, & CRF100F, 92-09
M318-4	XL/XR/TLR 125-200, 79-03
M328-4	XL/XR 250-350, 78-00; XL/XR350R 83-85; XR200R, 84-85; XR250L, 91-96
M320-2	XR400R, 96-04
M221	XR600R, 91-07; XR650L, 93-07

M339-8	XL/XR 500-600, 79-90
M225	XR650R, 00-07

Twins

M321	125-200cc Twins, 65-78
M322	250-350cc Twins, 64-74
M323	250-360cc Twins, 74-77
M324-5	Twinstar, Rebel 250 & Nighthawk 250, 78-03
M334	400-450cc Twins, 78-87
M333	450 & 500cc Twins, 65-76
M335	CX & GL500/650, 78-83
M344	VT500, 83-88
M313	VT700 & 750, 83-87
M314-3	VT750 Shadow Chain Drive, 98-06
M440	VT1100C Shadow, 85-96
M460-4	VT1100 Series, 95-07
M230	VTX1800 Series, 02-08
M231	VTX1300 Series, 03-09

Fours

M332	CB350-550, SOHC, 71-78
M345	CB550 & 650, 83-85
M336	CB650,79-82
M341	CB750 SOHC, 69-78
M337	CB750 DOHC, 79-82
M436	CB750 Nighthawk, 91-93 & 95-99
M325	CB900, 1000 & 1100, 80-83
M439	600 Hurricane, 87-90
M441-2	CBR600F2 & F3, 91-98
M445-2	CBR600F4, 99-06
M220	CBR600RR, 03-06
M434-2	CBR900RR Fireblade, 93-99
M329	500cc V-Fours, 84-86
M349	700-1000cc Interceptor, 83-85
M458-2	VFR700F-750F, 86-97
M438	VFR800FI Interceptor, 98-00
M327	700-1100cc V-Fours, 82-88
M508	ST1100/Pan European, 90-02
M340	GL1000 & 1100, 75-83
M504	GL1200, 84-87

Sixes

M505	GL1500 Gold Wing, 88-92
M506-2	GL1500 Gold Wing, 93-00
M507-2	GL1800 Gold Wing, 01-05
M462-2	GL1500C Valkyrie, 97-03

KAWASAKI

ATVs

465-2	Bayou KLF220 & KLF250, 88-03
M466-4	Bayou KLF300, 86-04
M467	Bayou KLF400, 93-99
M470	Lakota KEF300, 95-99
M385-2	Mojave KSF250, 87-04

Singles

M350-9	80-350cc Rotary Valve, 66-01
M444-2	KX60, 83-02; KX80 83-90
M448-2	KX80, 91-00; KX85, 01-10 & KX100, 89-09
M351	KDX200, 83-88
M447-3	KX125 & KX250, 82-91; KX500, 83-04
M472-2	KX125, 92-00
M473-2	KX250, 92-00
M474-3	KLR650, 87-07
M240	KLR650, 08-09

Twins

M355	KZ400, KZ/Z440, EN450 & EN500, 74-95
M360-3	EX500, GPZ500S, & Ninja 500R, 87-02
M356-5	Vulcan 700 & 750, 85-06
M354-3	Vulcan 800 & Vulcan 800 Classic, 95-05
M357-2	Vulcan 1500, 87-99

M471-3	Vulcan 1500 Series, 96-08

Fours

M449	KZ500/550 & ZX550, 79-85
M450	KZ, Z & ZX750, 80-85
M358	KZ650, 77-83
M359-3	Z & KZ 900-1000cc, 73-81
M451-3	KZ, ZX & ZN 1000 &1100cc, 81-02
M452-3	ZX500 & Ninja ZX600, 85-97
M468-2	Ninja ZX-6, 90-04
M469	Ninja ZX-7, ZX7R & ZX7RR, 91-98
M453-3	Ninja ZX900, ZX1000 & ZX1100, 84-01
M409	Concours, 86-04

POLARIS

ATVs

M496	3-, 4- and 6-Wheel Models w/250-425cc Engines, 85-95
M362-2	Magnum & Big Boss, 96-99
M363	Scrambler 500 4X4, 97-00
M365-3	Sportsman/Xplorer, 96-08
M367	Predator 500, 03-07

SUZUKI

ATVs

M381	ALT/LT 125 & 185, 83-87
M475	LT230 & LT250, 85-90
M380-2	LT250R Quad Racer, 85-92
M483-2	LT-4WD, LT-F4WDX & LT-F250, 87-98
M270-2	LT-Z400, 03-08
M343	LT-F500F Quadrunner, 98-00

Singles

M369	125-400cc, 64-81
M371	RM50-400 Twin Shock, 75-81
M379	RM125-500 Single Shock, 81-88
M386	RM80-250, 89-95
M400	RM125, 96-00
M401	RM250, 96-02
M476	DR250-350, 90-94
M477-2	DR-Z400E, S & SM, 00-08
M384-4	LS650 Savage/S40, 86-07

Twins

M372	GS400-450 Chain Drive, 77-87
M484-3	GS500E Twins, 89-02
M361	SV650, 1999-2002
M481-5	VS700-800 Intruder/S50, 85-07
M261	1500 Intruder/C90, 98-07
M260-2	Volusia/Boulevard C50, 01-08
M482-3	VS1400 Intruder/S83, 87-07

Triple

M368	GT380, 550 & 750, 72-77

Fours

M373	GS550, 77-86
M364	GS650, 81-83
M370	GS750, 77-82
M376	GS850-1100 Shaft Drive, 79-84
M378	GS1100 Chain Drive, 80-81
M383-3	Katana 600, 88-96 GSX-R750-1100, 86-87
M331	GSX-R600, 97-00
M264	GSX-R600, 01-05
M478-2	GSX-R750, 88-92; GSX750F Katana, 89-96
M485	GSX-R750, 96-99
M377	GSX-R1000, 01-04
M266	GSX-R1000, 05-06
M265	GSX1300R Hayabusa, 99-07
M338	Bandit 600, 95-00
M353	GSF1200 Bandit, 96-03

YAMAHA

ATVs

M499-2	YFM80 Moto-4, Badger & Raptor, 85-08
M394	YTM200, 225 & YFM200, 83-86
M488-5	Blaster, 88-05
M489-2	Timberwolf, 89-00
M487-5	Warrior, 87-04
M486-6	Banshee, 87-06
M490-3	Moto-4 & Big Bear, 87-04
M493	Kodiak, 93-98
M285-2	Grizzly 660, 02-08
M280-2	Raptor 660R, 01-05
M290	Raptor 700R, 06-09

Singles

M492-2	PW50 & 80 Y-Zinger & BW80 Big Wheel 80, 81-02
M410	80-175 Piston Port, 68-76
M415	250-400 Piston Port, 68-76
M412	DT & MX Series, 77-83
M414	IT125-490, 76-86
M393	YZ50-80 Monoshock, 78-90
M413	YZ100-490 Monoshock, 76-84
M390	YZ125-250, 85-87 YZ490, 85-90
M391	YZ125-250, 88-93 & WR250Z, 91-93
M497-2	YZ125, 94-01
M498	YZ250, 94-98; WR250Z, 94-97
M406	YZ250F & WR250F, 01-03
M491-2	YZ400F, 98-99 & 426F, 00-02; WR400F, 98-00 & 426F, 00-01
M417	XT125-250, 80-84
M480-3	XT350, 85-00; TT350, 86-87
M405	XT/TT 500, 76-81
M416	XT/TT 600, 83-89

Twins

M403	650cc Twins, 70-82
M395-10	XV535-1100 Virago, 81-03
M495-6	V-Star 650, 98-09
M281-4	V-Star 1100, 99-09
M282	Road Star, 99-05

Triple

M404	XS750 & XS850, 77-81

Fours

M387	XJ550, XJ600 & FJ600, 81-92
M494	XJ600 Seca II/Diversion, 92-98
M388	YX600 Radian & FZ600, 86-90
M396	FZR600, 89-93
M392	FZ700-750 & Fazer, 85-87
M411	XS1100, 78-81
M461	YZF-R6, 99-04
M398	YZF-R1, 98-03
M399	FZ1, 01-05
M397	FJ1100 & 1200, 84-93
M375	V-Max, 85-03
M374	Royal Star, 96-03

VINTAGE MOTORCYCLES

Clymer® Collection Series

M330	Vintage British Street Bikes, BSA 500-650cc Unit Twins; Norton 750 & 850cc Commandos; Triumph 500-750cc Twins
M300	Vintage Dirt Bikes, V. 1 Bultaco, 125-370cc Singles; Montesa, 123-360cc Singles; Ossa, 125-250cc Singles
M305	Vintage Japanese Street Bikes Honda, 250 & 305cc Twins; Kawasaki, 250-750cc Triples; Kawasaki, 900 & 1000cc Fours